simply delicious food
morning noon and night

simply delicious food
morning noon and night

150 recipes for every time of day

FRAN WARDE

PHOTOGRAPHY BY DEBI TRELOAR

RYLAND
PETERS
& SMALL

LONDON NEW YORK

Senior Designer	Louise Leffler
Food Editor	Elsa Petersen-Schepelern
Editors	Maddalena Bastianelli
	Jenni Muir
Index	Hilary Bird
Production	Patricia Harrington
Location Researcher	Kate Brunt
Art Director	Gabriella Le Grazie
Publishing Director	Alison Starling
Food Stylist	Fran Warde
Food Stylist's Assistant	Janet Dalzel Piper
Stylists	Emily Chalmers
	Abigail Aherne
	Karina Garrick
Photographer's Assistants	Lina Ikse Bergman
	Brian Benson

First published in United States in 2000
by Ryland Peters & Small Inc.
150th West 56th Street, Suite 6303
New York, NY 10019

10 9 8 7 6 5 4 3 2 1

Text © Fran Warde 2000
Design and photographs © Ryland Peters & Small 2000

Printed and bound in China by Toppan Printing Co.

ISBN 1 84172 091 7

A catalog record for this book is available from the Library of Congress.

notes

All spoon measurements are level unless otherwise stated.

All fruits and vegetables should be washed thoroughly and peeled in the usual way, unless otherwise advised. Carrots in particular should be peeled, topped, and tailed, and apples and pears should be cored before juicing. Unwaxed citrus fruits and cucumbers should be used whenever possible.

Remember that pregnant women, very young children, the elderly, or the infirm should avoid eating raw or partially cooked eggs and soft or blue cheeses.

Speciality Asian ingredients are available in larger supermarkets, Indian, Thai, Chinese, Japanese, and Vietnamese stores, and Asian supermarkets.

Grills, grill pans, broilers, and ovens should be preheated to the required temperature before adding the food. If using a convection oven, decrease the cooking times according to the manufacturer's recommendations.

contents

introduction

Cooking is a joy, and eating is a pleasure, so my kitchen is a happy sanctuary. From the age of two I was allowed to cook at home. Ok, I can hear my mother calling me an "assistant mess maker", chucking flour here and there, pouring half the sugar in the bowl and the other half on the counter, squeezing butter through my fingers, but it was fun and certainly much better than playing in sand as all the textures were different and we could eat what we made.

Gardening was also important in my family and just about everything was homegrown. My summers were spent picking peas and shelling them, gathering runner beans and slicing them with a very old-fashioned slicer, cutting lettuces and washing them, and digging and peeling carrots. I would sit amongst the strawberries and raspberries, pluck them straight from the plant, and pop them into my eager little mouth. We climbed apple, pear, and plum trees, gathering the plumpest fruits which we would share with our donkey and my guinea pigs. It was fun, but also the start of my appreciation of good fresh food. We would watch it grow, then gather it to cook and serve at the table for a comforting family meal—I loved it.

I hope that I have the same patience as my mother had with me when it comes to teaching my two boys this most wonderful of basic life skills. We all need to eat, and the best food is home cooked and made from good fresh produce.

What started in my formative years as playtime and a game has continued to follow me through life. Catering college beckoned, then off I went to the Café Royal in London, all bright-eyed and bushy-tailed, I left 18 months later feeling

You must be able to laugh in your kitchen and share the triumphs, as well as those moments when you do not achieve perfection, with ease and happiness. Cooking should be one of life's pleasures. We all need food to thrive, and the better the food the better we live. It is a joy to eat a freshly cooked meal, prepared with thought, consumed with an enjoyable drink, and taken in good company.

very sad and despondent, so I decided to take another tack. First I cooked my way around Britain and the Mediterranean. Then the other side of the world beckoned and off I went. It was fantastic. I landed in Australia with just $500, which was not a lot, even 15 years ago. My Australian friends were kind but I needed to work. Luckily the fusion food trend was beginning there and I was intrigued, excited, and fascinated—all my senses exploded. The time spent in Australia was hugely important to my culinary education and my brain was working overtime storing and gleaning information.

One of the craziest things I have ever done was to set off to sea one night on a small fishing boat out of Darwin, with four guys I had only just met. I had always wanted to see fish at its best, so that later in life I could say with authority "That is not fresh!" It was the best and worst eight days of my life. I was scared and couldn't find my sea legs, but the fish, shrimp, and crayfish were fantastic and I got to swim with dolphins. It was the most informative fish course that I have ever been on. Learning all about fish and how to store and fillet them from a fisherman is a privilege and I had no need to be scared. I eventually found my sea legs and went back to sea for another three weeks!

When I returned to London I just cooked and cooked. Ideas were falling out of my head and the adrenaline was whizzing around my body. While working as a caterer I was offered an exciting opportunity to open a restaurant with a friend. We had a small fixed menu as well as a large roving menu that changed according to the produce available and what we felt like cooking.

I loved cooking in the restaurant: orders pouring in, temperatures rising, working as a team, customers waiting, praise being given, pots being washed, the kitchen being cleaned, and tomorrow's menu being planned for it all to start again. I thrived on it but eventually left and moved into writing and teaching.

As you will see from this book, my food is eclectic and gathered from all over the world. It's very hard to describe my style of cooking exactly, but I think of it as enjoyable to prepare and delicious to eat. You must be able to laugh in your kitchen and share the triumphs, as well as those moments when you do not achieve perfection, with ease and happiness. My basic principles of good cooking are as follows:

Go shopping and choose what is fresh, seasonal, and looks so good that you simply have to buy it. That may be because of its color, smell, texture, or simply a yearning you have to handle and taste it.

Cook with passion, pleasure, kindness, and interest. When preparing your feast, keep it simple and don't hesitate to stay within your abilities—if you overstretch and stress yourself in the kitchen you will only become frustrated. Cooking should be one of life's pleasures. We all need food to thrive, and the better the food we eat, the better we live.

The final essential part of good cooking is the eating. It is a joy to eat freshly cooked food, prepared with thought, consumed with an enjoyable drink, and taken in good company. This will always be one of life's most important and sociable skills, therefore I say life should be "Simply Delicious!"

menu planner

V - suitable for vegetarians

Breakfast and Brunch
V Fruit Platter, 31
V House Granola, 17
V Boiled Egg and Toasted "Soldiers," 17
  Kedgeree with Poached Eggs, 35
V Panettone French Toast with
    Cinnamon and Bananas, 37
V Plum and Apricot Compote, 17
  Smoked Salmon Bagels with Poached
    Eggs, 22
V Swiss Muesli, 21
  "The Works," 21

Soups
V Bouillabaisse, 129
V Butternut and Cashew Soup, 130
V Gazpacho, 87
V Green Bean and Herb Broth, 131
  Rich Tuscan Bean Soup, 119

Snacks
V Blue Cheese and Tomato Crostini, 101
V Cheese on Toast, 179
  Cheese-Stuffed Croissants, 87
  Farmhouse Sauté with Bacon and
    Onions, 179
V French Toast with Fried Tomatoes, 180
V Garlic Bread, 76
V Garlic Toast, 47
  Ham and Thyme Tortilla, 96
V Mushrooms on Toast with Scrambled
    Eggs, 180
  Mountain Eggs, 100
V Toasted Ciabatta Pizzas, 53
V Turkish Toasted Bread, 158
V Zucchini and Cheddar on Toast, 99

Sandwiches, Wraps, and Rolls
  Chicken Salad Wrap, 89
V Cucumber Sandwiches, 103

V Egg and Watercress Rolls, 104
  Focaccia with Broiled Chicken, 96
V Hummus and Salad in Turkish
    Flatbread, 95
  Steak and Tomato Sandwich, 95

Party Nibbles
  Avruga Baby Baked Potatoes, 137
  Chinese Duck Forks, 141
V Crispy Noodles, 138
V Goat Cheese and Pepper Crostini, 141
V Parmesan Wafers, 137
  Mexican Shrimp Wraps, 141

Salads
V Asparagus and Roasted Peppers, 67
V Avocado and Chickpea Salad, 125
V Bean and Mint Salad, 158
  Chicken Liver Salad, 72
V Chickpea, Tomato, and Pepper Salad, 58
V Feta, Onion, and Cucumber Salad, 75
V Leaf and Herb Salad, 59
V Mozarella Cheese with Fennel and
    New Potatoes, 69
V Panzanella, 69
V Potato and Watercress with Mustard
    Seeds, 70
  Roasted Butternut, Tomato, and
    Prosciutto Salad, 73
V Salad Box, 88
  Salade Niçoise, 122
V Spanish Roast Pepper Salad, 166
  Spinach and Bacon Salad with Dijon
    Dressing, 112
V Summer Beans and Couscous
    Salad, 66
V Summer Salad, 47
V Summer Vine Tomato Salad, 69
V Warm Mediterranean Puy Lentil
    Salad, 70

morning

I love my bed, so breakfast has to be really good to entice me to get out of it. During the week, wake me with a mug of steaming fresh coffee and a bowl of granola. But give me a lazy weekend and I want to ease myself into the day with an indulgent yet civilized breakfast of fresh juices and fruits, sizzling bacon, poached eggs, thick-cut toast with melting butter and jelly, tea, cranberry and orange muffins, and newspapers to read slowly. Make time this weekend for yourself, celebrate breakfast, and feel fantastic. Then, when you find life needs a mid-morning sweetener, try freshly baked banana bread or irresistible coffee and walnut cake with tea or coffee, the height of comfort food. When you want to share an elegant brunch with friends and family, serve a spicy Bloody Mary and French toast made with panettone, hot bananas, and cinnamon. Relax and lounge the morning away, slowly eating and talking—pure bliss.

quick and healthy breakfasts tea know-how Sunday morning celebration

coffee know-how something sweet…with coffee weekend brunch

quick and healthy breakfasts

Breakfast is an important meal, but there never seems to be enough time to enjoy it. Everyone—including me—would rather spend longer in bed. However, you should try to make time for breakfast as it will set you up for the rest of the day. Prepare one of these quick and easy dishes to make sure the day's first meal is delicious and nutritious.

Plum and apricot compote

Eat lots of fruit every day as part of a healthy diet. Make a batch of fruit compote, then store it in the fridge ready to serve every morning with a bowl of granola. You can cook this compote on top of the stove or bake it in the oven. I prefer the latter because the fruit seems to hold its shape better.

If you like spices, stir ½ teaspoon of apple pie spice, ground cinnamon, or freshly grated nutmeg into the compote before cooking. Vanilla extract or the grated zest of an orange or lemon is also delicious.

1 lb. plums, halved and pitted, about 6
1 lb. apricots, halved and pitted, about 10
⅔ cup brown sugar
Serves 4

Put the prepared fruit in an ovenproof dish, sprinkle with the sugar, then add ¾ cup water. Cover and cook in a preheated oven at 350°F for 30 minutes until the fruit is tender and the juice is syrupy.

House granola

After tasting this you will forget all other granolas, and feel virtuous knowing that you really did make your own breakfast. Store in an airtight container for up to 4 weeks—if it lasts that long.

4 cups rolled oats
⅓ cup whole almonds
⅓ cup raisins
5-6 ready-to-eat dried apricots, chopped
⅓ cup pumpkin seeds
¼ cup raw sugar
¼ cup maple syrup

a non-stick baking tray
Serves 4

Mix all the ingredients together in a large bowl, then transfer to the baking tray. Bake in a preheated oven at 325°F for 25 minutes, until toasted.

Remove from the oven and stir well. Return the mixture to the oven and cook for a further 15 minutes until the granola is crisp and light golden.

Remove from the oven. Eat while hot with milk, or let cool, then transfer to an airtight container and store.

Breakfast blitz

This drink is pure nutritional heaven. Thanks to the growing popularity of vegetable juices, juice extractors are becoming more affordable—soon every keen cook and healthy eater will own one. Make sure you buy organic produce for juicing; it is important not to peel the vegetables and fruit as key vitamins are stored just below the skin.

2 apples, cored
2 beets, trimmed
2 carrots, trimmed
2 celery stalks
1 inch fresh ginger, peeled
Serves 4

Put the fruit and vegetables into the juicer and extract the juice according to the manufacturer's instructions. Pour into glasses and serve immediately.

Boiled egg and toasted "soldiers"

This deliciously simple breakfast is a winner every time. The secret is to serve the egg perfectly cooked, with thick strips of hot buttered toast (known as soldiers) for dunking.

4 free-range eggs, at room temperature
4 slices bread
unsalted butter, for spreading
sea salt and freshly ground black pepper
Serves 4

Fill a small saucepan with water and heat until barely simmering. Lower the eggs, on a spoon, into the water and let them simmer for 3–4 minutes for soft-cooked, 5–6 minutes for medium-cooked, or 8–9 minutes for hard-cooked eggs.

Meanwhile, toast the bread, spread with butter, and cut into 4 or 5 strips or "soldiers." Serve with the eggs and small piles of sea salt and freshly ground black pepper. To eat, dip the toast into the egg—just perfect!

top tip: To avoid cracked shells, use eggs that are at room temperature and gently lower them on a spoon into barely simmering water. Simmer rather than boil and don't let them jostle around in the pan.

Growing, harvesting, and roasting

Tea leaves come from an Asian evergreen shrub that grows abundantly in China, India, Sri Lanka, Japan, Indonesia, East Africa, Latin America, and Russia. Good growing conditions are essential for the fine flavor of a tea. The plants favor a hot, humid climate with warm winters that are not too dry. Most important however is the altitude, which needs to be around 6000 feet above sea level to produce a fine and fragrant tea with good color.

Tea is an every-hour, everyday drink in Europe and America, whereas in China and Japan it forms an important part of cultural life and "tea ceremonies" feature as part of social customs and traditions. When it first arrived in the West, tea was mostly associated with the aristocracy, but once it became more readily available, it was popular at every level of society.

Teas are classified according to the quality of leaves picked from the shrub; the younger the leaf, the better the tea. Broken larger leaves are used in lesser teas. The leaves are treated in different ways to make various types of tea:

Green tea is an unfermented leaf, but roasted immediately after harvesting to give a very clear infusion with a delicate taste. It is very popular in China and Japan. Varieties include Gunpowder, Gen Mai Cha, Lung Ching, and Sencha. Just a little pinch is needed to make a cup of green tea, otherwise the flavor will be too strong.

Black tea is fermented and dried, giving an infusion with a strong taste and rich amber color. It is the most common type of tea and there are many different varieties to choose from, including Assam, Darjeeling, Lapsang Souchong, and Superior Orange Pekoe. Go to a specialist store and taste some samples: the differences are really quite amazing.

potted perfection
tea

Oolong tea is a semi-fermented leaf—fragrant with a sweet aftertaste. Grown in Taiwan and very popular in America, there are eight grades ranging from choicest to common. Try Fancy Grade Oolong, which gives a mellow infusion best drunk without milk.

Scented tea comes in many varieties, the most famous of which is Earl Grey, a black tea with oil of bergamot added. Other scented teas may have flowers, fruit, leaves, stems, or roots added to create the fragrance.

Herbal teas are also called tisanes because they do not contain any real tea leaves. There are many varieties, such as camomile, jasmine, lemongrass, peppermint, and raspberry, and they can be drunk hot or cold.

Stored in a dark place, tea can be kept for a year. I think it is important to have a lovely teapot that pours well. Some people will only drink tea out of china mugs or cups—this is for you to choose. In my view, tea is all too often made in a mug, which is fine for green tea and herbals, but black and oolong teas really require the space of a teapot to brew properly.

Making black, oolong, or scented tea

Always use freshly boiled filtered water. Rinse out the teapot with the boiled water, then add the tea, allowing 1 teaspoon per person and one for the pot. Pour in the boiled water and leave to infuse for 3–5 minutes. Do not over-infuse the tea or it will become bitter and dark.

How strong and what to add, if anything, is a matter of personal taste. Tea can be drunk black, or with a dash of cold milk; some people take sugar and others a slice of lemon. I like it very weak and black—a simple, pure infusion.

Making green and herbal tea

These can be made in a mug for one person but if you are making for any more, use a teapot. Green tea is best weak so calculate ½ teaspoon of tea per person, and the same for herbal. Many herbal teas come in individual bags and one of these per person is the best ratio. Brew for 1 minute—no longer or it will become bitter, then drink without milk or sugar.

Sunday morning celebration

Lazy weekend breakfasts are so good. I love that special feeling when time seems to stand still and the fast—often chaotic—pace of weekday life slows right down. Why not start the day with a cup of tea or coffee in bed to wake you gently from your slumber, then head to the kitchen to create one of these extra-special breakfasts?

Swiss muesli

This soft granola is steeped overnight in creamy yogurt, then served topped with delicious summer berries and honey.

2⅔ cups rolled oats
1½ cups bran flakes
½ cup dried apple pieces
½ cup raisins
⅔ cup unsweetened shredded coconut
½ cup chopped toasted hazelnuts
¼ cup sunflower seeds
2 cups plain yogurt

To serve
4 cups mixed fresh berries, such as
  blueberries, raspberries, and strawberries
¼ cup honey
Serves 4

Mix all the dry ingredients in a large bowl. Add the yogurt, mix well, cover, and chill overnight.

Serve in bowls with a scattering of berries and the honey drizzled over the top.

Plum pastries

Fill these easy pastries with your favorite fruit and nuts. Croissant dough, found in the chiller cabinets at large supermarkets, freezes well, so you can make freshly baked pastries any time you want.

1 can chilled ready-to-bake croissant dough,
  about 8 oz.
6 plums, halved and pitted
4 teaspoons honey
1 tablespoon slivered almonds

a baking tray, oiled
Makes 6

Remove the dough from the can, unravel it, and flatten. Cut along the perforations to make 6 rectangles and lay well apart on the baking tray.

Put 2 halves of fruit on each piece of dough, then drizzle with honey and sprinkle with the almonds.

Bake in a preheated oven at 350°F for about 15–20 minutes until puffed and golden. Remove from the oven and serve hot or cold.

Cranberry and orange muffins

I can hear you shouting: "Who has time to make these?!" But I can assure you they don't take long. Send the family out for a jog or to walk the dog and, while they're away, turn on the radio and get baking. They'll thank you for these lovely muffins.

1½ cups self-rising flour
1 cup plus 2 tablespoons sugar
1 teaspoon cinnamon
2 oranges
1 cup sour cream
4 tablespoons butter, softened
1 egg, lightly beaten
1½ cups fresh cranberries

a 12-hole deep muffin pan, lined with
  8 muffin paper cases
Makes 8

Sift the flour into a bowl, then stir in the sugar and cinnamon.

Grate the zest from the oranges and reserve. Slice off the white pith, then cut down between the membranes to release the segments.

In a second bowl, beat the sour cream with the butter, egg, and orange zest until smooth. Add to the dry ingredients and mix gently.

Add the cranberries and orange segments and fold gently into the mixture using as few strokes as possible. Do not beat or overmix; the batter should look slightly streaky.

Spoon the mixture into the prepared muffin cases, filling each one to about two-thirds full.

Bake in a preheated oven at 350°F for about 35 minutes until golden and firm to the touch. Remove from the oven and eat warm with butter and a cup of coffee or tea.

top tip: To check if the muffins are cooked, insert a skewer, toothpick, or the tip of a pointed knife into the center of one muffin: it should come out clean. If not, continue baking for 5 more minutes.

"The works"

An indulgent breakfast unlike traditional fried versions. It is cooked primarily in the oven and packed with flavor, not grease.

4 top-quality sausages
4 medium cremini mushrooms
4 slices bacon
2 large tomatoes, halved
2 tablespoons sunflower oil
4 free-range eggs
4 slices whole-wheat bread
butter, for spreading

a large baking tray, lightly oiled
Serves 4

Arrange the sausages and mushrooms on the baking tray, spaced well apart, and cook in a preheated oven at 350°F for 15 minutes. Turn the sausages and mushrooms, add the bacon and tomatoes, return to the oven, and cook for a further 15 minutes.

Heat the oil in a non-stick skillet, add the eggs, then cover and cook for 2 minutes, or until the surface of the eggs becomes opaque.

Meanwhile, toast the bread and spread with butter. To serve, put the toast on 4 heated plates, top with the eggs, and add the sausages, bacon, mushrooms, and tomatoes.

Smoked salmon bagels with poached eggs

Here is a light alternative to a fried breakfast—and it is so easy to make. For me, smoked salmon and poached eggs are truly delicious and a real luxury. Treat yourself to this wonderful breakfast or, better still, get your partner to make it for you.

4 bagels
butter, for spreading
4 oz. watercress or arugula
8 oz. smoked salmon
4 eggs
sea salt and freshly ground black pepper
a bunch of chives, to serve
Serves 4

Cut the bagels in half, toast them, then spread lightly with butter. Top with watercress or arugula, folds of salmon, and a twist or two of black pepper.

Crack the eggs into 4 cups. Bring a large saucepan of water to a boil and, when simmering, stir the water around in one direction to create a whirlpool. Gently slip each egg into the water, return to a gentle simmer, and cover with a lid. Remove the saucepan from the heat and let stand for 6 minutes.

Remove the eggs with a slotted spoon and drain on folded paper towels. To serve, put the eggs on top of the bagels, then add the chives.

For a change, try scrambled eggs. Put 5 eggs, 5 tablespoons milk, and a pinch of salt in a bowl and beat with a fork. Heat 2 tablespoons butter in a non-stick skillet, pour in the egg mixture, and stir with a wooden spoon until the eggs are almost set to a soft, creamy scramble. To serve, spoon the eggs on top of the prepared bagels.

Melon and strawberry juice

These summer fruits, now available all year round, make a delicious, refreshing drink. Juice them for breakfast or serve instead of tea.

1 melon, such as cantaloupe or honeydew
2 cups strawberries, hulled
juice of 2 limes
8 ice cubes, plus extra to serve
Serves 4

Chop the melon flesh into small pieces and put in a blender with the strawberries, lime juice, and ice. Blend until smooth and serve in a large chilled pitcher.

top tip: For a flavored yogurt drink, add some natural yogurt to the blender with the fruit.

Super juice

A pure, clean-tasting drink for a special breakfast treat.

1 medium pineapple, or 2 cans pineapple chunks in
    natural juice, 8 oz. each
3 large bananas, sliced
1 cup cranberry juice
8 ice cubes
Serves 4

If using fresh pineapple, top and tail it, cut away the skin, and remove all the dark prickly spots. Cut the pineapple into quarters lengthwise, then remove the core from each section. Chop the fruit and put into a large pitcher. Add the bananas, cranberry juice, and ice, then blend with a stick blender until there are no lumps. Serve in chilled glasses.

coffee

the coffee knowledge

Growing, harvesting, and roasting

Coffee plants grow in sub-tropical climates around the world. The fruit looks similar to cherries but over 6–9 months will ripen to a very dark brown. Each "cherry" contains two coffee beans which are removed by drying, soaking, or husking of the cherry flesh. The beans are then sorted and bagged to be transported.

At their destination, the beans are roasted. Roasting caramelizes the sugars and carbohydrates in the bean and produces that distinctive aroma and flavor we all love. How the beans are roasted will effect the flavor of the coffee. Dark-roasted beans have a rather sharp, acidic flavor, good for espresso, whereas lightly roasted beans have less caffeine and acidity and are best used in coffee presses or filters.

Blending and grinding

Blending is a complex art, but also a matter of taste. If you go to a specialist coffee merchant, they will make a blend to suit your very own personal taste—experiment with different brands and blends and beans from different parts of the world until you find the perfect cup for your household.

The beans are ground according to the method you use to make your coffee: use coarsely ground coffee for a percolator, medium grind for a drip filter or coffee press, and fine grind for espresso machines. For really good, fresh coffee, try to grind your own beans—the flavor is much richer. Keep the beans in an airtight container in the fridge. If you must buy your coffee ready-ground, buy only what you need for the week and store it in the refrigerator.

Making coffee

As a rough guide, use 2 level tablespoons of freshly ground coffee per cup if using a coffee press, drip filter, or espresso machine. Rinse the coffee press out with hot water, add the coffee, and fill with hot water. Let steep for 3 minutes then gently push the plunger. Follow the manufacturer's directions for espresso machines. If you prefer white coffee, serve it with scalded milk for a real treat.

something sweet…with coffee

Banana bread

I discovered this amazing cake in a coffee bar in Queenstown, New Zealand. It was so good that I had to have a second piece.

1 cup (2 sticks) butter, softened
1 cup plus 2 tablespoons sugar
2 eggs, lightly beaten
2 large bananas, mashed, about 1 cup
2½ cups self-rising flour, sifted
⅓ cup milk
1 teaspoon vanilla extract

a loaf pan, 9½ x 5½ x 3½ inches, greased and lined with waxed paper
Serves 8

Cream the butter and sugar in a bowl until light and creamy, then add the beaten eggs, a little at a time, mixing well between each addition. Mix in the mashed banana and fold in the flour. Add the milk and vanilla and mix until smooth.

Pour into the loaf pan and bake in a preheated oven at 350°F for 50 minutes.

Let cool in the pan for 10 minutes, then turn out onto a wire rack to cool completely.

Oat bars

Who can resist these sweet, sticky treats? As a variation, add golden raisins or raisins and some chopped pecans, walnuts, or hazelnuts to the mixture before baking.

1 cup (2 sticks) butter, softened
¾ cup light corn syrup
¾ cup dark brown sugar
5⅓ cups rolled oats

a rectangular baking pan,
    12 x 7½ x 2 inches, lightly greased
Makes 12

Put the butter, syrup, and sugar in a saucepan and melt over a low heat, mixing well. Add the oats and stir until evenly coated.

Tip the mixture into the prepared baking pan. Using a round-bladed knife, push the mixture into the corners and level the surface.

Bake in a preheated oven at 400°F for about 15 minutes, until golden brown.

Remove from the oven, let cool for 5 minutes, then cut into squares or rectangles. Let cool in the pan for a further 10 minutes.

Remove from the pan and serve with a cup of hot frothy coffee or freshly brewed tea.

Coffee and walnut cake

No coffee break is complete without a slice of cake to recharge energy levels. This one will keep you going until lunchtime.

1 cup (2 sticks) butter, softened
1¼ cups sugar
4 eggs, lightly beaten
5 teaspoons instant coffee granules
1⅔ cups self-rising flour, sifted
1 cup walnut halves

Coffee buttercream

½ cup (1 stick) butter, softened
3 cups confectioners' sugar, sifted, plus extra for dusting
3 teaspoons instant coffee granules

2 round, 6-inch baking pans, lightly greased and lined with waxed paper
Serves 4–6

Put the butter and sugar in a bowl and, using a wooden spoon or electric beater, beat until pale and creamy. Beat in the eggs, a little at a time, until the mixture is light and fluffy.

Dissolve the coffee in 5 tablespoons hot water, then stir into the butter and egg mixture. Using a large metal spoon, fold in the flour.

Divide the mixture evenly between the baking pans and level the surface. Bake in a preheated oven at 350°F for about 20–25 minutes until the cake is golden and a skewer inserted in the middle comes out clean. If it doesn't, bake for a further 5–10 minutes, then test again. Remove from the oven.

Let cool in the pans for 5 minutes, then turn out onto a wire rack to cool completely.

To make the buttercream, beat the butter and confectioners' sugar in a bowl until smooth and fluffy. Dissolve the coffee in 2 tablespoons hot water and mix into the buttercream.

To assemble the cake, lightly dust a plate with confectioners' sugar and put one of the cakes on the plate. Spread it with half the buttercream and top with the other cake. Spread the remaining buttercream on top and make a pattern in it with a fork. Decorate with the walnut halves. This cake is best eaten the day it is made.

top tip: To prevent the cake mixture from curdling when beating in the eggs, add 1 tablespoon of the flour after each addition of egg.

When you need an energy boost, something sweet and homemade is best, so never let your cake tin or cookie jar sit empty. These recipes will inspire you to start baking and fill the pantry with mid-morning treats that are just as delicious mid-afternoon.

weekend brunch

Brunch is a wonderful way to entertain. The day is still young and it's the weekend, so everyone has a great lounging feeling. Mix a few drinks, get in the newspapers and chat about the week's happenings while you slowly eat your way into the day.

Kick-starter Bloody Mary

If you or your guests can't face alcohol so early in the day, it is a good idea to make two pitchers of this drink—one with everything and the other without the vodka.

5 lemons
1 cup vodka
3 inches white horseradish, freshly grated, or 1 tablespoon bottled horseradish
1 tablespoon Worcestershire sauce
1 teaspoon Tabasco sauce
lots of freshly ground black pepper
3 cups tomato juice, well chilled
celery stalks, with leaves, to serve

Serves 4

Half fill a large pitcher with crushed ice. Cut 1 lemon into slices and squeeze the juice from the others. Add to the pitcher, together with all the other ingredients except the celery. Mix well. Serve in highball glasses with a celery stalk.

Fruit platter

Everyone loves fruit, especially if it's all
been prepared for them and looks stunning.
This one is always a brunch winner.

1 ripe melon, such as orange cantaloupe or
   green honeydew
2 papayas
4 limes, 2 juiced, 2 halved
2½ cups mixed berries, such as blackberries,
   blueberries, raspberries, red currants,
   and strawberries

Honey Yogurt
2 cups plain yogurt, preferably thick
⅓ cup honey
Serves 4

Peel, halve, and seed the melon, then cut into
thin wedges. Divide between 4 plates. Peel,
halve, and seed the papaya, cut into wedges,
then slice crosswise. Add to the melon. Sprinkle
with lime juice, then add the berries.

Put the yogurt in a bowl, drizzle with the honey,
and serve with the fruit and halves of lime.

Spiced muffins

These easy-to-make muffins are packed with aromatic spices. Chopped fruit keeps them deliciously moist while the maple syrup adds a smoky, sticky sweetness.

1²⁄₃ cups self-rising flour, sifted
³⁄₄ cup plus 2 tablespoons raw sugar
¹⁄₄ teaspoon cinnamon
¹⁄₄ teaspoon freshly grated nutmeg
¹⁄₂ cup milk
1 egg, lightly beaten
3 tablespoons peanut oil
1 apple, cored and chopped, about 1³⁄₄ cups
2 bananas, chopped, about 1 cup
10 teaspoons maple syrup

a 12-hole deep muffin pan, lined with
   10 paper cases
Makes 10

Mix the flour, sugar, cinnamon, and nutmeg in a large bowl, then make a well in the center.

In a small bowl or pitcher, mix the milk, egg, and oil, then pour into the well you have made in the dry ingredients. Stir quickly with a wooden spoon until mixed, being careful not to overmix.

Fold in the chopped apple and bananas, then spoon the mixture into the prepared paper cases, filling each one to about two-thirds full.

Make a hollow in the top of the muffins with the back of a teaspoon and add 1 teaspoon of maple syrup to each one—don't worry if it drizzles out.

Bake in a preheated oven at 350°F for 20 minutes. Remove from the oven and serve immediately, or cool on a wire rack.

top tip: Cooking the muffins in pretty paper cases prevents the mixture sticking to the pan and helps each muffin keep its shape. They will also look special for your guests.

At the weekend, invite your friends over for a relaxing brunch and give them a feast. I always think brunch should be served on Sundays so that you can calmly prepare for it the day before. Buy fresh fruit and other food from the market and gather bunches of brightly colored flowers—this is all part of the fun.

To add a touch of style to your brunch party, lay the table with your best white, tablecloth and use your lovely china, silver, and glasses. Float flower petals in a glass bowl filled with water, or stand large sculptured-looking flowers, such as lilies, in a tall vase. Finally, to create a relaxed atmosphere and stylish setting, remember to keep everything simple, clean, and natural.

Kedgeree with poached eggs

For fish lovers everywhere, this old-fashioned British dish will be extremely satisfying. Smoked haddock (finnan haddie) is the traditional fish for kedgeree, but other kinds, such as smoked trout, are also good.

14 oz. undyed smoked haddock, cod, trout, or whitefish
¾ cup long-grain rice
2 cups baby spinach leaves, trimmed and washed
4 large eggs
grated zest and juice of 1 lemon
4 tablespoons butter
sea salt and freshly ground black pepper
a bunch of chives, chopped

an ovenproof dish, lightly buttered
Serves 4

Put the smoked fish in the ovenproof dish, in a single layer, skin side down and cover with foil. Cook in a preheated oven at 350°F for about 10 minutes. Remove from the oven and let cool a little. When cool enough to handle, flake the fish and carefully remove and discard any bones and skin.

Put the rice in a saucepan and add enough water to cover the rice by 1 inch.

Bring to a boil, then cover and simmer for 12 minutes. (Do not remove the lid during cooking.) Let stand for a few minutes before removing the lid, then stir in the spinach and cook for 1 minute. Drain well.

To poach the eggs, crack the 4 eggs into 4 cups. Bring a large saucepan of water to a boil and, when simmering, stir the water around in one direction to create a whirlpool. Gently slip each egg into the water, return to a gentle simmer, then cover, remove from the heat, and let stand for 6-7 minutes, depending on how cooked you like the yolks.

Meanwhile, gently mix the poached fish flakes with the rice, lemon zest and juice, butter, salt, and pepper. Spoon the mixture into a lightly buttered dish, cover, and keep it warm.

Remove each egg from the pan with a slotted spoon. Use folded paper towels to absorb any excess water from under the spoon. Put the eggs on top of the rice, sprinkle with the chives, and serve.

top tip: If you do not like smoked fish, use a mixture of fresh salmon and shrimp instead. It makes a truly delicious alternative.

Panettone French toast with cinnamon and bananas

This sweet, fruity bread is a speciality of Italy and traditionally eaten at Christmas, but I think it's far too good to restrict to the festive season. Fortunately, you can now buy it all year round in Italian stores.

4 eggs
3 tablespoons light cream
1 teaspoon ground cinnamon, plus extra for dusting
4 thick slices panettone
⅓ cup butter
4 bananas
maple syrup, to serve
Serves 4

Put the eggs, cream, and cinnamon in a bowl and beat with a fork. Pour into a shallow, flat-bottomed dish, add the slices of panettone, and let soak for 5 minutes. Turn them over and let soak on the other side for 5 minutes.

Heat the butter in a large, heavy, cast-iron or nonstick skillet. When the butter is foaming, drain off the excess egg mixture from the panettone and add the soaked slices to the skillet. Cook for 4–5 minutes on each side or until golden.

Put the cooked panettone on a heated serving plate and keep it warm in a low oven. Slice the bananas into the skillet and toss gently for 5 minutes. Spoon them over the top of the panettone, then drizzle with the maple syrup and dust with cinnamon. Serve hot as soon as possible.

After brunch it's time to settle into a comfortable chair and enjoy a sumptuous creamy coffee while flicking through the magazine section of the paper. Your contented guests can leave at their leisure, or stay on for more chatting, some wine, or perhaps a walk in the park. Leave the dishes as long as you like: we were not meant to work on Sundays.

Café frappé

A real treat—café frappé is very refreshing and makes a great change from regular coffee. I prefer this drink made with good instant coffee (to me it gives it a smoother flavor and velvety texture), but if you prefer real coffee, make it in the usual way and use 2 tablespoons for this recipe.

3⅔ cups whole milk, chilled
⅓ cup heavy cream, chilled
2 tablespoons instant coffee granules
12 ice cubes
Serves 4

Mix the milk and cream in a pitcher or bowl, then put in the freezer for about 3 hours until frozen. Chill 4 glasses in the freezer until cold.

Put the instant coffee in a cup with 1 tablespoon boiling water. Stir to dissolve the granules, then cool and chill.

Put the frozen creamy milk, coffee, and ice cubes in a blender and blend until smooth.

Pour into the chilled glasses and serve at once.

If you do not like coffee, try making crushed tea. Simply make a pot of weak tea such as Earl Grey, jasmine, green tea, or one of your favorites. Cool the tea and put it in the freezer to chill. Fork through the tea every 20 minutes to break up the large ice crystals that form. When firm and icy, spoon the mixture into chilled glasses and top with sliced peaches or orange wedges. This also makes an exotic light dessert to finish off an indulgent meal.

top tip: To give your frappé a kick, add a dash or two of rich coffee liqueur such as Kahlúa—it's heaven, but for adults only.

noon

What a glorious time of day, with the sun high in the sky and lunch about to begin. This is my favorite meal—after a busy morning my tummy is yearning for food. The best lunches in my view are always those eaten on holiday or at weekends when the atmosphere is relaxed and indulgent and a long, slow meal with wine can gently drift into the afternoon. Lunch can be taken anywhere and in any style but the one necessity is time: it is very important to sit down and eat slowly, to talk with friends and enjoy yourself. Busy people often take lunch on the move or, as I like to say, on the hoof. This is not the most relaxing way to eat, but in modern society it is a fact of life. Please don't let your midday meal be a bag of chips. With some planning and just a little bit of effort the night before, a great packed lunch that is fresh and healthy can be made to brighten your day and provide good nourishment.

beach barbecue family picnic garden lunch summer salads winter salads

winter lunch Saturday family lunch classic Sunday roast working lunch

food on the move snack attack teatime

Whisk me off to a sunny beach and I am happy, surrounded by friends, family, children playing, and sand between my toes. I like to sip a white wine spritzer as I light the fire, have a dip in the sea while the coals get hot, then return to cook a delicious but easy lunch in the open air. A favorite choice is crab spaghetti with chile mussels accompanied by crisp salad and crunchy garlic toast drizzled with olive oil. Afterwards, we simply lie back and breathe in the happiness.

beach barbecue

Crab spaghetti with chile mussels

This deliciously simple dish can be made on a grill or by building a safe fire. Don't forget to take two saucepans and a colander.

½ cup olive oil
1 onion, chopped
2 garlic cloves, crushed and chopped

1¾ cups canned chopped tomatoes, 14 oz.
1 glass white wine, about ⅔ cup
1 mild red chile, seeded and finely chopped
14 oz. spaghetti, fresh or dried
14 oz. cleaned fresh mussels
about 1 cup fresh crabmeat
juice of 1 lemon
a bunch of flat-leaf parsley, coarsely chopped
sea salt and freshly ground black pepper
Serves 4

Heat half the olive oil in a medium saucepan over the hot coals. Add the onion and garlic and cook until softened and translucent.

Add the chopped tomatoes, white wine, chopped chile, salt, and pepper. Mix well, bring to a boil, and simmer for about 10 minutes to reduce and thicken the sauce.

Bring a large saucepan of water to a boil, add the spaghetti and push it down into the water. Stir to separate the strands and stop them sticking together. Cook for about 9 minutes, or until *al dente* (cooked, but "firm to the tooth.")

Meanwhile, discard any open mussels that will not close when tapped sharply with a knife. Add the mussels to the sauce, mix well, then cover with a lid and simmer for 4 minutes.

Drain the spaghetti into a colander. Add the remaining olive oil to the same pan, then gently stir in the crabmeat, lemon juice, and chopped parsley. Add the drained spaghetti, return to the heat, and toss well to mix all the ingredients.

Serve the spaghetti in piles with spoonfuls of chile mussels and sauce on top.

top tip: Try to buy a dressed crab, readily available in supermarkets, food halls, and from fish stores by the sea. Cooking a fresh, raw crab is very simple, but extracting the meat can be a long, slow process. With a dressed crab the fiddly work is done for you, and it tastes much better than canned crab.

top tip: If any mussels remain unopened after cooking, it may be that there was not enough heat generated in the saucepan. Make sure the pan is boiling and covered. If any of the mussels still do not open, discard them.

Eating under the sun surrounded by nature is wonderful, but it is important to take all the necessary equipment for the barbecue so you can enjoy your day fully. Make a list and double-check that you have all that is needed for the perfect day out. Don't throw the list away either: I promise this day will be so special that you will want to repeat it soon.

Lightly drizzle the garlic-flavored bread with olive oil and sprinkle with sea salt before serving hot.

top tip: Try using different breads for garlic toast. It is delicious made with a loaf of farmhouse white, whole-wheat, soda, or sourdough bread, not just baguette.

Summer salad

A quick and simple salad with the good, clean, peppery taste of watercress and the delicious crunch of radish and celery.

10 oz. watercress, ends trimmed
a bunch of radishes, trimmed and halved, about 10
6 celery stalks, sliced
¼ cup olive oil
2 tablespoons balsamic vinegar
sea salt and freshly ground black pepper
Serves 4

Put the watercress in a salad bowl, then add the halved radishes and sliced celery.

Drizzle with the olive oil. Add the vinegar, salt, and pepper, toss well, and enjoy.

top tip: Some salad items are not good travelers and, by the time they make it from your shopping basket to the table, they may have seen better days. Replace any of the ingredients in the above salad with whatever is fresh and best in the market on the day: remember shopping should always be flexible.

Garlic toast

No one can resist thick slices of crunchy hot toast topped with garlic and extra virgin olive oil.

4 thick slices of your favorite bread
1 large garlic clove
extra virgin olive oil, to serve
sea salt
Serves 4

Toast the bread on each side. Rub one side of each piece with the peeled garlic clove, letting the toasted bread act as a grater, and catching the small bits of garlic.

Damper with red berry salad

To me this is real summer outdoor cooking and eating. We used to make these sticks of bread endlessly as kids and dip them into big pots of homemade strawberry jelly.

5 cups seasonal red berries
¼ cup sugar
1 cup self-rising flour
2 tablespoons butter, cut into small pieces
½ cup milk or water
heavy cream or clotted cream, to serve

8 wooden satay sticks, rubbed with butter at one end
Serves 4

Put half the berries in a medium bowl, add half the sugar, and coarsely crush the fruit with the back of a fork. Stir in the remaining berries and set aside.

Put the flour in a second medium bowl. Add the butter and use your fingers to rub it into the flour until the mixture is smooth. Add the remaining sugar and liquid and mix well until the mixture sticks together and forms a dough.

Divide the dough into 8 pieces and shape them into sausages around the end of the buttered sticks. Cook over the whitened embers of a grill or fire for approximately 15 minutes, turning constantly. When cooked they should be lightly colored and firm.

Serve the damper on small plates with the crushed fruits spooned over and a dollop of cream alongside.

top tip: You can also cook the dough sticks on a baking tray in a preheated oven at 400°F for about 12–15 minutes.

White wine spritzer
A pretty spritzer to cool a hot brow.

1 bottle white wine, 3 cups, chilled
4 cups sparkling mineral water, chilled
2 cups frozen white grapes
Serves 8

Put the chilled white wine, mineral water, and frozen grapes in a large pitcher and mix well. Serve the spritzer in your favorite large glasses.

top tip: Frozen fruit cubes are great for chilling picnic drinks. They don't melt as quickly as ordinary ice cubes and children love eating them too. Try chopping up orange segments, putting them in ice cube trays, covering with a little fresh juice, then freezing them.

family picnic

When the weather is great, quickly gather some food and head to an open space to eat from your lap. Don't forget to take a book and a game or two so you can really make an afternoon of it. The menu here is perfect for a relaxed and enjoyable lunch.

top tip: Always remember to take a chopping board and a sharp knife with you on a picnic—it's much better to slice bread on arrival for real freshness, and these pizzas are best when they travel whole.

menu

Still ginger lemonade

Toasted ciabatta pizzas

Chicken and tarragon pesto pasta

Nutty toffee apples and toffee cherries

Still ginger lemonade

It is worth making a weekly batch of this drink as it is so refreshing and there is something rather satisfying about being served a good homemade lemonade.

4 inches fresh ginger, peeled and finely sliced
juice of 4 lemons
1 lemon, sliced
6 tablespoons sugar
Serves 4

Put the ginger, lemon juice, sliced lemon, and sugar in a heatproof pitcher. Add 4 cups boiling water. Mix well and let steep for 2 hours. Chill, then serve poured over ice.

top tip: Many variations can be made on this drink. If you don't like lemons, use limes or oranges and, for a really clean taste, add mint. If you want something stronger, add a shot of vodka to each glass.

Toasted ciabatta pizzas

Many kinds of bread can be used in these fantastic pizzas. You can also use blue cheese, Monterey Jack, or Cheddar instead of mozzarella.

1 loaf ciabatta, split lengthwise or sliced
1 garlic clove, peeled
about ¼ cup olive oil
4 ripe tomatoes, peeled and sliced
a handful of pitted olives
a bunch of marjoram
10 oz. mozzarella cheese
a bunch of basil
sea salt and freshly ground black pepper
Serves 4

Broil the ciabatta under a hot broiler until lightly toasted, then rub with garlic, using it like a grater. Put the garlic ciabatta on a baking tray and drizzle with a little of the olive oil.

Arrange the sliced tomatoes on the bread, then add the olives, marjoram, mozzarella, basil, salt, and pepper. Drizzle some more oil over the top.

Cook in a preheated oven at 350°F for about 15-20 minutes until the tomatoes are softened and crisp round the edges and the mozarella has melted. Remove, let cool, and wrap in waxed paper before packing.

Chicken and tarragon pesto pasta

This really is a great dish—tarragon and chicken go together so well. Kids will love it, yet it tastes good enough for adults to tuck into as well. Pesto can be made out of most herbs, so don't hesitate to try your favorites in this recipe and blend to create your own version. We eat a lot of this one at home: it's scrumptious.

10 oz. dried penne pasta
½ cup olive oil
1 cup freshly grated Parmesan cheese
½ cup pan-toasted pine nuts
a large bunch of tarragon, leaves stripped from the stem and chopped
grated zest and juice of 1 lemon
1 garlic clove, crushed and chopped
3 cooked chicken breasts, sliced
2 packages fresh arugula, about 4 oz.
sea salt and freshly ground black pepper

Serves 4

Bring a large saucepan of water to a boil. Add the pasta, stir, and cook for 8–9 minutes, until *al dente* ("firm to the tooth.") When cooked, drain and refresh the pasta in cold water, then drain thoroughly and toss in half the olive oil.

Put the Parmesan, pine nuts, tarragon, lemon zest and juice, garlic, and remaining oil in a bowl and work until smooth with a stick blender.

Put the pasta, pesto, chicken, and arugula in a serving bowl, season, and toss well, coating the pasta and chicken evenly with the pesto.

top tip: If you do not want meat, replace the chicken with steamed vegetables such as zucchinis, sugar snap peas, fava beans, or runner beans.

top tip: When taking this salad on a picnic, don't add the arugula until just before eating or the oil will make it wilt.

For sophisticated parkland grazing, supplement your cooking with wedges of juicy fresh melon, salty slivers of prosciutto crudo, chunks of piquant salami or chorizo, some mouthwatering olives, an oozy cheese and some crunchy hazelnut biscotti. Pack in a crate for easy transportation and don't forget the beer.

Nutty toffee apples and toffee cherries

Your dentist will not be happy with this recipe but I can assure you that you will be.

2 cups sugar
20 cherries, with stalks
4 apples
²⁄₃ cup chopped nuts

Serves 4

Put the sugar in a small saucepan with ¾ cup water and bring to a boil. Reduce the heat and simmer until golden. Don't use a spoon to stir the mixture, just swirl the pan: this keeps the heat even and stops the sugar from crystalizing.

When the caramel is golden, remove the pan from the heat. Holding the stems, quickly dip the cherries into the hot caramel, then put them on a sheet of waxed paper to set.

Spear the apples onto forks. Add the nuts to the caramel and heat through briefly if it is stiff. Dip the apples in the mixture, swirling them around until they are coated all over with the nutty caramel. Put on the waxed paper to set for about 5 minutes. Don't let the apples or cherries touch each other or they will stick together.

Wrap the apples and cherries separately in sheets of waxed paper for transportation.

When the weather is good I can't resist eating outside and, for a special celebration, it's such fun to do it in grand style. Pull the table into the garden and bring out the chairs. Decorate with pretty napkins, flowers and foliage, candles—don't stop. For maximum conviviality, put all the food out for friends and family to help themselves, then settle down to eat, drink, and soak up the atmosphere.

garden lunch

Rosemary and lemon roasted chicken

In a simple dish such as this, quality ingredients are important. Choose an organic or free-range chicken, unwaxed lemons, a good Modena balsamic vinegar, and extra virgin oil. It really makes a difference.

4 lb. chicken pieces or 1 chicken, about 3½–4 lb.*
3 lemons, cut into wedges
leaves from a large bunch of rosemary
3 red onions
3 oz. large black olives (about 10–12), pitted
¼ cup balsamic vinegar
2 tablespoons extra virgin olive oil
sea salt and freshly ground black pepper
Serves 4

If using chicken pieces, trim off any excess fat and put the pieces in a large bowl. Add the lemon and rosemary.

Cut the onions in half lengthwise, leaving the root end intact. Cut the halves into wedges and add to the chicken.

Add the olives, balsamic vinegar, olive oil, and seasoning and mix well to coat the chicken with the flavorings.

Cover and let stand at room temperature for 1 hour, or in the refrigerator overnight.

Put the chicken in a large roasting pan and arrange the marinade ingredients around it. Cook in a preheated oven at 375°F for 30 minutes. Turn the chicken pieces thoroughly in the pan to ensure even cooking and coloring, then cook for a further 30 minutes.

Remove the chicken from the oven. Using a slotted spoon, lift out the chicken, lemon, onions, and olives and put them on a serving dish.

Skim the cooking juices, discarding the fat. Pour the juices over the chicken and serve hot or at room temperature.

*Note: If using a whole chicken, lay the bird on its back. Use a large knife to cut through the skin between the leg and breast of the chicken, then bend the leg backwards until the joint cracks. Cut through the joint to separate the leg. Repeat on the other side.

Bend the drumsticks back away from the thighs to crack the joints, then cut through with the knife to separate. Bend back the wings of the chicken and cut through the joints near each breast to separate.

Put the bird on its side and use scissors or poultry shears to cut from the leg joint up along the backbone to the neck. Repeat along the other side. (Wrap the backbone and store for use in stock another day.)

Hold the chicken breast-side down and bend it back to crack the breastbone. Use the scissors to cut along each side of the breastbone and remove the breasts.

Chickpea, tomato, and pepper salad

I have a passion for chickpeas (garbanzo beans), but have found that most people don't really know what to do with them. Using the canned variety, as in this super Mediterranean-style salad, dispenses with the soaking that is needed with dried beans.

5 plum tomatoes, halved and seeded
3 large red bell peppers, halved and seeded
2 cups canned chickpeas, rinsed and drained
a bunch of flat-leaf parsley
sea salt and freshly ground black pepper
extra virgin olive oil, to serve
Serves 4

Lightly oil a roasting pan and add the tomatoes and bell peppers. Cook in a preheated oven at 375°F for 20 minutes.

Remove from the oven and transfer the tomatoes and peppers to a bowl. Add the drained chickpeas, then mix in the parsley and seasoning.

Transfer the salad to a serving dish, sprinkle with a little olive oil, then serve at room temperature.

Leaf and herb salad

This may be a simple salad, but simplicity is best when you are working with the fragrant flavors of herbs. To make it extra pretty, garnish with edible flowers such as heartsease, nasturtiums, and pansies when available.

10 oz. mixed leaves, or 1 head of lettuce
a handful of edible flowers (optional)

4 bunches of herbs, such as basil, chives, marjoram, flat-leaf parsley, sage, tarragon, fennel, and lovage
about ¼ cup Delicious Vinaigrette (page 61)

Serves 4

Wash and trim the mixed leaves or lettuce as necessary. Tear into a bowl. Add the edible flowers, if using, and a selection of your chosen herbs. Drizzle with the vinaigrette and toss well to coat all the leaves. Serve immediately.

Let the sky be full of sun and your table full of delicious food! Laying all the dishes out at once is easy on the cook but also a sure way to get the conversation and laughter flowing freely while guests help themselves and each other. Graze in leisurely fashion, nibbling happily, as the day wears on, and empty bottles of wine mount up.

Baked eggplants with pesto sauce

If you can find them, use the little Asian eggplants to make this dish—they look very pretty and have a more interesting texture than large eggplants. When buying herbs, try going to independent stores or market stalls where they are sold like bunches of flowers—I find these herbs taste better and are much better value.

10 oz. small eggplants
¼ cup olive oil

Pesto
a large bunch of basil
1 cup pan-toasted pine nuts
1 garlic clove
1 cup freshly grated Parmesan cheese
about ½ cup olive oil
sea salt and freshly ground black pepper

a baking tray, lightly oiled
Serves 4

Cut the eggplants in half lengthwise and put on the baking tray. Drizzle with a little of the olive oil and cook in a preheated oven at 375°F for about 15-20 minutes, then turn them over and cook for a further 15 minutes.

To make the pesto, put the basil, pine nuts, garlic, Parmesan, the remaining olive oil, and seasoning in a blender and purée until smooth. When the eggplants are cooked, drizzle with pesto and serve hot or cold.

top tip: Make twice the quantity of pesto and store the extra in the fridge—it always comes in handy as an easy salad dressing or tossed through pasta for a quick, delicious supper. Keep the pesto covered with a thin film of olive oil and it will stay fresh for several weeks.

Delicious vinaigrette

Using a stick blender gives such a thick texture to this vinaigrette that it clings to the salad leaves. Children love it—give them bread or vegetable sticks for dipping. Store any leftovers in an airtight bottle in a cool dark place (but not the fridge).

½ cup white wine vinegar
juice of ½ lemon
2 teaspoons Dijon mustard
2 teaspoons whole-grain mustard
1 teaspoon sugar
1 cup olive oil or vegetable oil
sea salt and freshly ground black pepper
Serves 4

Put the vinegar, lemon juice, mustards, sugar, and some salt and pepper in a pitcher. Mix with a stick blender, or beat by hand.

While still blending, slowly pour in the oil. When it has all been incorporated, you will have a fantastic emulsion. If it seems too thick, just add a little water and blend again.

Nectarine tart

The combination of crumbly, sweet pastry tart and slivers of juicy nectarines makes for a sensational blend of delicate summer flavors. Come fall, don't hesitate to use plums.

1²/₃ cups all-purpose flour
1 cup plus 2 tablespoons butter, cut into small pieces
1 cup confectioners' sugar, plus extra for dusting
2–3 egg yolks
10–12 nectarines or peaches, about 3 lb.
vanilla ice cream, to serve

a 9-inch false-bottom tart pan
Serves 6–8

Put the flour, butter, and confectioners' sugar in a food processor and blend until the mixture resembles fine breadcrumbs. Add the egg yolks and blend again until it forms a dough ball.

Wrap the pastry in plastic and chill in the refrigerator for at least 30 minutes.

Roll out the chilled pastry into a large circle at least 2 inches wider than the base of the tin.

Use the rolling pin to help you carefully lift up the pastry and lay it over the top of the tart pan.

Gently press the pastry down into the pan, making sure there are no air pockets, then use a sharp knife to trim off the excess pastry. Chill the tart shell for 15 minutes.*

Cut the nectarines or peaches in half, twist to remove the pits, then cut the fruit into slices.

Remove the chilled tart shell from the fridge and, working from the outside, arrange the nectarine or peach slices in circles on the pastry, until all the fruit has been used.

Bake in a preheated oven at 375°F for 30 minutes, then reduce the heat to 300°F and cook for 40 minutes until the fruit is tender and golden and the pastry is crisp.

Dust the tart all over with confectioners' sugar then serve hot or cold with scoops of good-quality vanilla ice cream.

*Note: This pastry is very fragile, but don't despair. Just line your tart pan as best you can, and then add extra pieces of pastry to patch up any cracks or holes.

top tip: Instead of vanilla ice cream, serve with a generous dollop of strained yogurt drizzled with honey; or clotted cream; sour cream, or sweetened fromage frais. Use small tart pans, about 3 inches in diameter, to make individual tarts.

Espresso granita

A refreshing end to a meal on a warm summer's day. Good biscotti can be found in Italian and other gourmet stores.

2 tablespoons sugar
3 tablespoons freshly ground coffee
To serve
biscotti
light cream (optional)

Serves 4

Put 4 small glasses or espresso cups in the freezer to chill. Put the sugar and coffee in a coffee press. Add 4 cups boiling water and let stand for 5 minutes to develop the flavor. Plunge the press, pour the coffee into a heatproof pitcher and let cool before chilling in the fridge.

When very cold, pour the coffee into a bowl and freeze for 20 minutes, until ice crystals form around the edge. Crush the crystals with a fork and return to the freezer. Repeat about 3 times to form an even mixture of fine ice crystals.

Cover and return to the freezer until ready to serve. Serve the granita in the serving glasses or cups with a biscotti and a drizzle of cream for anyone who prefers their coffee white.

Mini chocolate brownie squares

Everyone loves brownies—rich, sticky, and chocolaty, the perfect morsel to finish off any delicious meal. They are wonderful too, served with a cup of coffee the next day.

4 oz. good-quality bitter chocolate
½ cup (1 stick) unsalted butter
2 eggs, beaten
1 cup plus 2 tablespoons sugar
⅔ cup self-rising flour
⅓ cup pecans, chopped (optional)

a rectangular cake pan, 11 x 7 inches, lined with waxed paper
Makes about 54

Put the chocolate and butter in a large saucepan and melt over a low heat. Remove from the heat, add the eggs, sugar, flour, and pecans, if using, and mix well. Pour into the prepared cake pan, smooth over the surface, and bake in a preheated oven at 350°F for 30 minutes.

Remove from the oven and let cool in the pan. When cool, lift the slab of brownies out of the pan using the waxed paper, then cut into small squares.

top tip: There are more brownies in this recipe than you will need for one lunch party but they will keep for several days in an airtight container, providing you can control your intake. For a truly wicked but sensational quick dessert, take a tub of good vanilla ice cream, a basket of raspberries, and half the brownies. Let the ice cream soften a little, then spoon it into a mixing bowl. Add the raspberries and chopped brownies, mix gently, then return to the freezer for 20 minutes before serving.

Eating in the garden makes the most of heady floral fragrances and warm summer light. Shake out that crisp, linen tablecloth and wrap the silver in napkins. Use nature's Eden to decorate your table: gather small bunches of seasonal herbs and flowers and loosely tie them with a piece of bear grass. Lay out plump bunches of grapes and fill beautiful old plates with sugared almonds to serve with tea and coffee. It is these little touches that will make your lunch party so special and individual.

summer salads

When the markets and stores are overflowing with fresh summer produce, there is no meal quite as beautiful to look at, or as deliciously tasty, as a salad. Glossed with a mouthwatering dressing (even if it's only a little fine oil and lemon), the crisp textures, vibrant colors, and wonderfully juicy flavors are ample temptation to make a healthy salad every day—so go on! Here are some ideas to get you started.

Summer beans and couscous salad
A great dish on its own, this also makes a lovely accompaniment to Rosemary and Lemon Roasted Chicken (page 58).

1 cup couscous
1 cup shelled and peeled fava beans or green beans, chopped
1 cup shelled green peas, fresh or frozen
1 cup sugar snap peas, trimmed
1 cup chopped runner beans
grated zest and juice of 2 lemons
⅓ cup olive oil
2 teaspoons Spanish sweet paprika
1 garlic clove, crushed and chopped
sea salt
Serves 4

Put the couscous in a bowl, cover with boiling water, mix well, and let stand for 10 minutes until swollen.

Bring a large saucepan of water to a boil, then add the fava beans or green beans and cook for 5 minutes. Add the sugar snap peas and runner beans and cook for a further 3 minutes. Drain and refresh under cold running water until the vegetables are cold (otherwise they will lose their bright fresh color).

Drain the couscous. Transfer to a large bowl and add the beans and peas, lemon juice and zest, olive oil, paprika, garlic, and salt. Mix well, then serve.

Asparagus and roasted peppers

You can make this salad on a grill or grill pan, or by roasting the vegetables in the oven. Take your pick—I prefer using a grill pan.

3 red bell peppers
2 red onions
1 lb. asparagus, trimmed
1/3 cup olive oil
2 tablespoons balsamic vinegar
sea salt and freshly ground black pepper
2 oz. Parmesan cheese, cut into shavings, to serve (optional)

Serves 4

Cut the bell pepper flesh away from the core in flat pieces to make grilling easier. Put the pepper skin-side down on a preheated grill pan and cook until the skin is blistered and turning black.

Transfer the peppers to a small bowl and cover—they will continue cooking and be easier to peel. When cool, peel the skins away from the silky flesh.

Cut the onions into wedges leaving the root end intact to hold them together. Add to the grill pan and cook for 4 minutes on each side. Add the asparagus and cook for 3-4 minutes or until just soft.

Put the peppers in a bowl with the onions, asparagus, olive oil, vinegar, salt, and pepper. Toss to coat, then serve with shavings of Parmesan, if desired.

Mozzarella cheese with fennel and new potatoes

Mozzarella made with buffalo milk (often called *mozzarella di bufala*) has a much creamier, softer texture than mozzarella made from cow's milk. Although buffalo mozzarella is more expensive, I always use it in preference to the cow's milk variety.

7 oz. new potatoes, about 12–15
1 head Florence fennel
7 oz. mozzarella cheese
½ cup olive oil
¼ cup balsamic vinegar
sea salt and freshly ground black pepper

Serves 4

Cook the potatoes in a large saucepan of boiling water until just tender, about 12–14 minutes depending on their size. Drain and let cool. When the potatoes are cold, cut them in half and set aside until needed.

Trim the fennel, then cut into halves or quarters. Cut out and discard the hard central core. Using a sharp knife or a mandoline, slice the fennel very finely and set aside.

Slice the mozzarella into thin rounds.

Arrange the potatoes, fennel, and mozzarella in stacks on 4 serving plates, seasoning generously between each layer with salt and pepper.

Drizzle the salads with the olive oil and sprinkle with balsamic vinegar just before serving.

Panzanella

When I find some particularly delicious bread, I always buy too much. This Tuscan salad, better made with day-old bread, is the perfect way to use up the leftovers.

4 slices country bread, cubed
4 ripe tomatoes, cut into wedges
6 inches cucumber, peeled and cut into chunks
1 red onion, sliced
a bunch of flat-leaf parsley, coarsely chopped
⅔ cup olives, pitted
2 tablespoons capers
¼ cup olive oil
1½ tablespoons wine vinegar
juice of ½ lemon
1 teaspoon sugar
sea salt and freshly ground black pepper

Serves 4

Put the bread cubes in a large bowl with the tomato, cucumber, onion, and chopped parsley.

Add the olives, capers, olive oil, vinegar, lemon juice, sugar, salt, and pepper, then mix well.

Leave the salad to stand for 1 hour before serving so that the bread soaks up the juices and all the flavors mingle.

top tip: This salad is highly flexible, so use whatever you have to hand—sourdough bread, a little garlic, a bunch of basil. Serve with broiled meat or fish for a hearty meal.

Summer vine tomato salad

Tomatoes vary so much. Sometimes they look fantastic but the flavor is a letdown, so it really is a case of tasting before you buy. This is not always possible, but my storekeeper lets me taste first because he knows that if I'm not happy I will complain.

8 oz. sweetest vine tomatoes
6 inches cucumber
⅓ cup pitted black olives
8 anchovy fillets
a large bunch of purple or green basil
8 oz. mozzarella cheese, sliced
⅓ cup olive oil
2 tablespoons balsamic vinegar
sea salt and freshly ground black pepper

a baking tray, lightly oiled
Serves 4

Put the tomatoes on the baking tray and cook in a preheated oven at 250°F for 1 hour. Transfer to a large salad bowl.

Peel the cucumber, cut in half lengthwise and, using a teaspoon, remove all the seeds. Cut each cucumber half into ½-inch slices. Add to the tomatoes with the olives and mix gently.

Cut the anchovy fillets into thin strips and add them to the salad bowl.

Tear the leaves from the bunch of basil and add to the bowl with the mozzarella, olive oil, vinegar, salt, and pepper. Toss well and serve.

winter salads

In cold weather the marriage of salad ingredients and warm vegetables is truly scrumptious. I love the way that the warmth of the cooked food makes the salad leaves soften, adding to the succulent mixture of piquant flavors.

Warm Mediterranean Puy lentil salad

Really, this is a salad for all seasons. It works wonderfully served warm or cold and is bound to become a regular feature on your table.

1 cup cherry tomatoes, about 10
1½ cups Puy lentils or other brown lentils
peeled rind and juice of 1 lemon
1 fresh bay leaf
2 garlic cloves, crushed and chopped
2 red onions, diced
½ cup pitted garlic olives
a bunch of flat-leaf parsley, coarsely chopped
¼ cup extra virgin olive oil
sea salt and freshly ground black pepper
4 oz. Parmesan or mozzarella cheese, sliced, to serve

a baking tray, lightly oiled
Serves 4

Put the cherry tomatoes on the baking tray and cook in a preheated oven at 250°F for 40 minutes.

Put the lentils in a saucepan. Add the lemon rind and juice, bay leaf, garlic, and enough water to cover. Stir, bring to a boil, then simmer for 40 minutes or until the lentils are soft.

Drain the lentils thoroughly and transfer to a large bowl. Add the tomatoes, red onion, olives, parsley, olive oil, salt, and pepper. Toss gently, then serve topped with slices of Parmesan or mozzarella.

top tip: This is not only a great salad but, with various additions, can also be served as a whole meal in endless ways. Try adding bacon or ham when cooking the lentils, or some spicy sausage just before you mix everything together.

Potato and watercress with mustard seeds

For a really stylish salad, I like to use blue or purple potatoes. They have a good waxy texture that I love. If they are unavailable, use another salad-type potato—any one of your favorites will do.

1 lb. small potatoes, unpeeled
2 teaspoons mustard seeds
¼ cup olive oil
1 tablespoon white wine vinegar
8 oz. watercress, ends trimmed
sea salt and freshly ground black pepper
Serves 4

Put the potatoes in a saucepan, cover with water, bring to a boil, then simmer for 12–14 minutes until done. Drain, then cut the potatoes into slices.

Crush the mustard seeds with a mortar and pestle, then mix in the olive oil, vinegar, and some salt and pepper. Pour the dressing over the potatoes and mix gently. Add the watercress, toss lightly, then serve.

Chicken liver salad

This salad makes a wonderful starter or supper dish. Be careful not to overcook the chicken livers, or they will become dry and tough, not juicy and soft. Chicken livers are available in butcher's shops and large supermarkets, fresh or frozen.

4 slices toasted or fried bread
8 oz. mixed lettuce leaves
8 oz. chicken livers
4 tablespoons butter
2 tablespoons olive oil
½ cup red wine
sea salt and freshly ground black pepper

Serves 4

Put the toast on 4 small salad plates and top with the lettuce leaves.

Trim the chicken livers, removing any tubes and any dark or slightly green patches. Cut the livers into equal pieces.

Melt the butter and olive oil in a large saucepan. When really hot, add the chicken livers and cook for 2 minutes on one side, then turn them over and cook for 2 minutes more.

Add salt and pepper, then carefully remove the livers from the saucepan, using a slotted spoon, and divide them between the plates, laying them on top of the lettuce leaves.

Add the wine to the pan juices and bring to a boil, stirring. Boil hard for 1 minute, then pour the hot dressing over the livers and serve.

Roasted butternut, tomato, and prosciutto salad

Butternut is the best-tasting pumpkin on the planet, especially when roasted. I don't remove the seeds as they are edible and taste good.

2 lb. butternut squash, unpeeled and cut into wedges

¼ cup olive oil

6 plum tomatoes, halved

12 slices prosciutto

2 packages fresh arugula, about 4 oz.

sea salt and freshly ground black pepper

2–3 tablespoons pumpkin oil, to serve (optional)

a baking tray, lightly oiled

Serves 4

Put the butternut on the baking tray, drizzle with the olive oil, and cook in a preheated oven at 350°F for 35 minutes or until softened and browned at the edges. Turn the wedges halfway through cooking so they roast evenly. Add the tomatoes to the tray for the last 15 minutes of cooking.

When cooked, remove the roasted butternut and tomatoes from the oven and divide them between 4 serving plates.

Lay the slices of prosciutto on the same baking tray and cook under a preheated broiler for 4 minutes on each side, or until the prosciutto is crisp and starting to brown.

Divide the arugula between the plates, putting it on top of the roasted butternut and tomatoes. Add the crispy prosciutto. Season with salt and pepper, drizzle with a little pumpkin oil, if using, then serve.

winter lunch

Recipes here can be served at any time, mid-week or weekend, but the emphasis is on gathering the family around the table for an informal but delicious meal. There are some treats in this section that take a little time to prepare, but most of the dishes are easy one-pot recipes.

menu

Feta, onion, and cucumber salad

Vegetable couscous

Lemon tart

Merlot

Feta, onion, and cucumber salad

Warm flatbread is a lovely accompaniment to this incredibly easy salad.

8 oz. feta cheese
6 scallions, sliced
7 inches cucumber
a bunch of dill, coarsely chopped
2 tablespoons olive oil
1 tablespoon wine vinegar
sea salt and freshly ground black pepper

Serves 4

Crumble the feta into a salad bowl, then add the sliced scallions.

Peel the cucumber, halve lengthwise, and scoop out the seeds with a teaspoon. Slice the halves into ½-inch pieces and add to the bowl.

Add the chopped dill, olive oil, vinegar, salt, and pepper. Toss the salad gently and serve.

Vegetable couscous

I think this is especially good for a large gathering of people, young and old. Don't be put off by the long list of ingredients—once in the pot, it looks after itself.

2 tablespoons olive oil
2 onions, cut into wedges
2 shallots, peeled
3 garlic cloves, crushed and chopped
1 fresh red chile, diced
1 teaspoon paprika
½ teaspoon ground cinnamon
½ teaspoon coriander seeds, crushed
½ teaspoon cumin seeds, crushed
4 cardamom pods, crushed
a large pinch of saffron threads
3 carrots, cut into 1-inch chunks
2 parsnips, cut into 1-inch chunks
½ butternut squash, cut into 1-inch chunks
2 zucchini, thickly sliced
2 cups canned peeled cherry tomatoes or whole plum tomatoes, 15 oz.
2½ cups vegetable stock

2 cups canned chickpeas, 15 oz., rinsed and drained
⅔ cup golden raisins
sea salt and freshly ground black pepper
a bunch of cilantro, chopped, to serve

Pine nut couscous

2½ cups couscous
1 cup pine nuts
4 tablespoons butter, melted

Serves 4

Heat the olive oil in a large saucepan. Add the onions, shallots, garlic, and chile and cook for 2 minutes. Add the paprika, cinnamon, coriander, and cumin seeds, cardamom, and saffron and cook for a further 3 minutes.

Add the carrots, parsnips, butternut, and zucchini. Cook for 5 minutes, stirring well to coat the vegetables with the spices.

Add the tomatoes, stock, chickpeas, golden raisins, salt, and pepper. They should be covered with liquid—add extra stock or water as necessary. Bring to a boil and simmer for 20 minutes.

Pour the couscous into a saucepan and add enough boiling water to cover it by 1 inch. Bring to a boil and simmer the couscous for 3 minutes, stirring frequently. Drain well.

Put the pine nuts in a dry skillet and cook over a medium heat, stirring constantly, until browned. Add to the drained couscous.

Pour the melted butter over the couscous and season with salt and pepper. Fluff up the grains with a fork and transfer to a large serving bowl.

Top the couscous with the cooked vegetable mixture and top with a generous quantity of chopped fresh cilantro. Serve hot.

top tip: Ready-ground spices lose their flavor quickly, so it is better to buy whole seeds and crush them as needed. A mortar and pestle makes this quick and easy to do.

Lemon tart

Just about everyone loves this easy classic.

Pastry

¾ cup all-purpose flour
4 tablespoons butter
2 tablespoons sugar
1–2 egg yolks

Lemon filling

2 eggs
¾ cup heavy cream
¼ cup sugar
grated zest and juice of 2 lemons
¼ cup confectioners' sugar, for dusting

a 9-inch false-bottom tart pan, greased
waxed paper and baking beans, pie weights, or uncooked rice

Serves 4

To make the pastry, put the flour, butter, and sugar in a food processor and pulse until the mixture resembles breadcrumbs. Alternatively, put in a mixing bowl and rub with your fingertips.

Add the egg yolk and mix to a dough. Wrap it in plastic wrap and chill for 30 minutes.

Roll out the pastry and gently line the tart pan. Prick the base all over with a fork, line the tart shell with waxed paper, and fill with baking beans.

Cook in a preheated oven at 400°F for about 30 minutes. Check after 12 minutes and reduce the heat if beginning to color.

Remove the tart shell from the oven, remove the waxed paper and baking beans, and reduce the oven temperature to 325°F.

To make the filling, beat the eggs in a large bowl, then mix in the cream, sugar, lemon zest, and juice. Pour into the tart shell and cook for 45–50 minutes or until the lemon filling has set.

Remove from the oven and dust evenly with confectioners' sugar. Put the tart under a very hot broiler and cook until all the sugar has caramelized. Let cool, then serve.

Saturday family lunch

Saturdays are often rushed affairs. It is a day that seems to be dedicated to catching up on shopping, washing, cleaning, a visit to the gym, or maybe recovering from that big Friday night. But please do make an effort to eat a good lunch. I have devised a simple-to-cook but great-to-eat meal just for your family and friends.

Garlic bread

Garlic bread is fantastic and children love it. Baguette is traditional but any bread works. Try farmhouse white, cottage loaf, ciabatta, Danish split, whole-wheat, mixed grain, or individual rolls and cut them accordingly.

1 loaf of bread
3 garlic cloves
½ cup (1 stick) butter, softened
a bunch of flat-leaf parsley, chopped
sea salt and freshly ground black pepper

a baking tray
Serves 4

Cut the bread into slices without cutting the crust all the way through, or cut it in half lengthwise.

Crush the whole cloves of garlic with the flat of a large knife, then peel, chop, and mash to a purée with a teaspoon of salt.

Mix the garlic purée, butter, parsley, salt, and pepper in a bowl, then spread generously onto the cut surfaces of the bread.

Wrap the bread in foil, put on a baking tray and cook in a preheated oven at 350°F for about 20 minutes. Serve hot with ratatouille.

Variation: For quick-style garlic bread, slice the loaf and toast it on one side. Spread the other side with garlic butter, then broil.

Ratatouille

All the vegetables for ratatouille must be fresh and full of flavor in order to show off this famous French dish at its best.

3 tablespoons olive oil, plus extra to serve
2 onions, chopped
2 garlic cloves, crushed and chopped
2 red bell peppers, seeded and cut into chunks
2 eggplants, cut into chunks
3 zucchini, thickly sliced
4 cups canned peeled plum tomatoes or passata (2 cans, 15 oz. each)
½ teaspoon dried oregano
½ teaspoon dried marjoram
a bunch of flat-leaf parsley or basil, chopped
sea salt and freshly ground black pepper
Serves 4

Heat the olive oil in a large saucepan. Add the chopped onion and garlic and cook, stirring, for 3 minutes without browning.

Add the bell peppers, eggplants, and zucchini to the pan and cook for 5 minutes, stirring frequently until the vegetables are lightly golden.

Add the canned tomatoes or passata, dried oregano, and marjoram. Season generously with salt and pepper and stir thoroughly.

Bring the mixture to a boil, then reduce the heat and simmer for 25 minutes, stirring occasionally.

Transfer the ratatouille to a large serving bowl. Sprinkle with the chopped parsley or basil, then drizzle with extra olive oil and serve.

top tip: Try making ratatouille the day before you plan to serve it. The flavor of the dish really seems to improve overnight and benefit from being cooled and reheated.

Upside-down pear cake

This dessert is very easy to make and great for children who want to help in the kitchen. Many types of fruit can be used in place of pears—try apples, bananas, peaches, pineapple, and plums.

3 pears, peeled, halved, and cored
¾ cup (1½ sticks) butter
¾ cup plus 2 tablespoons sugar
3 eggs
1 cup plus 2 tablespoons self-rising flour
3 tablespoons milk
1 tablespoon confectioners' sugar

a shallow cake pan, 8 inches diameter, greased
    and lined with waxed paper
Serves 4

Arrange the pear halves evenly over the bottom of the prepared pan and set aside.

Using an electric beater or a wooden spoon, cream the butter and sugar together in a large bowl until the mixture is light and fluffy.

Beat in the eggs, adding them one at a time and mixing well after each addition.

Add the flour to the bowl, gently fold it into the mixture, then stir in the milk.

Spoon the cake batter evenly over the pears and smooth the surface.

Cook in a preheated oven at 350°F for about 45 minutes, until the surface is firm when gently touched and the cake has slightly come away from the sides of the pan.

Remove from the oven, let cool for 5 minutes, then turn out onto a serving plate. Peel away the waxed paper, dust the top of the cake evenly with confectioners' sugar, and serve immediately.

classic Sunday roast

We all love the thought of a great family Sunday roast, particularly in winter. There is nothing better than to invite people round for a traditional, slow-paced meal, the kind of dinner that our parents and grandparents do so well. I love eating from a big table in the kitchen, so the cook never misses out on the conversation and, more to the point, everyone can help. Choose whichever roasted meat your family loves best—the roasting chart below is a ready-reckoner for whatever you plan to cook.

Roasting timetable

Use a meat thermometer to determine when your roast is done (see temperatures in brackets). Insert it into the thickest part of the meat without touching bone, then put on a roasting rack in a roasting pan. Put into a hot oven at 400°F for the first 20 minutes to seal in the juices and keep the meat succulent, then cook at 350°F.

Lamb
(internal meat temperature in brackets)

rare: 20 minutes per pound, plus 20 minutes (145°F)

medium: 25 minutes per pound, plus 25 minutes (160°F)

well done: 30 minutes per pound, plus 30 minutes (170°F)

Beef
(internal meat temperature in brackets)

rare: 20 minutes per pound, plus 20 minutes (145°F)

medium: 25 minutes per pound, plus 25 minutes (160°F)

well done: 30 minutes per pound, plus 30 minutes (170°F)

Pork
(internal meat temperature in brackets)

medium–well done: 25 minutes per pound, plus 25 minutes (160–170°F)

Chicken
(internal meat temperature in brackets)

20 minutes per pound, plus 20 minutes (175–180°F)

Turkey
(internal meat temperature in brackets)

25 minutes per pound, plus 25 minutes (175–180°F)

Venison
as for beef

Pheasant
as for chicken

Roasted pork with sage and apple

There are many good cuts of pork for roasting, but my favorite is a boned and rolled loin with the skin still attached to provide that all-important crackling. Ask the butcher to score the skin thoroughly for you before rolling and tying—this helps release the fat during cooking and makes the crackling crisp and dry. This recipe gives enough for four people plus some cold meat for the next day.

3 lb. top loin of pork, boned and rolled
2 lb. baking apples, peeled and cored
4 tablespoons butter
¼ cup hard cider
leaves from a bunch of sage, chopped
1 tablespoon all-purpose flour
2 cups vegetable stock or vegetable cooking liquid
sea salt

a heavy-bottom roasting pan with roasting rack
Serves 4

Just before cooking, sprinkle sea salt all over the pork skin and rub in well. Place on the roasting rack in the pan.

Roast in a preheated oven at 400°F for 20 minutes, then reduce to 350°F and cook for a further 1 hour.

Put the apples in a saucepan with the butter and cider. Cover with a lid and bring to a boil. Simmer the apples for 5 minutes, then add the chopped sage and remove the pan from the heat. Cover and set aside until needed.

When the pork is cooked, remove it from the roasting pan to a serving platter, cover with aluminum foil, and set aside in a warm place to rest for about 10 minutes.

Using a metal spoon, skim off any excess fat from the roasting pan. Put the pan over a medium heat on top of the stove. Add the flour and use a large spoon to stir it vigorously into the meat cooking juices,

Slowly add the vegetable stock (or the same quantity of any cooking liquid from vegetables boiled for lunch), and blend with a small whisk to give a smooth sauce.

Bring to a boil and simmer for 4 minutes. Season the gravy to taste then pour into a gravy boat and serve with the roast pork and sage-flavored apples.

menu 1
Roasted pork with sage and apple

Creamy mustard mash

Braised red cabbage

Chocolate pudding cake with raspberries

Chardonnay

menu 2
Lamb with rosemary and garlic

Roasted vegetables

Minted beans and peas

Lemon meringue pie

Pinot Noir

Lamb with rosemary and garlic

I like my lamb pink in the middle but if you don't, adjust cooking times according to the chart on page 79. Each piece of meat is different in weight, so do use a calculator to work out the exact roasting time.

1 leg of lamb, about 3 lb.

5 garlic cloves, sliced

5 sprigs of rosemary, broken into small sprigs

2 tablespoons honey

2 tablespoons Dijon mustard

1 tablespoon all-purpose flour

½ cup red wine

3 tablespoons redcurrant jelly

sea salt and freshly ground black pepper

a heavy-bottom roasting pan with roasting rack
Serves 4

Make incisions all over the lamb with a small, sharp knife. Insert a slice of garlic and a sprig of rosemary into each slit. Put the lamb on the rack in the roasting pan and cook in a preheated oven at 400°F for 20 minutes, then reduce to 350°F for 1 hour for rare meat.

Mix the honey and mustard together in a small pitcher. When the lamb has been roasting for 50 minutes, remove it from the oven and drizzle with the honey mixture. Return to the oven and roast for a further 10 minutes.

Remove the lamb from the oven, transfer to a carving board, cover with foil, and set aside for 10 minutes to let the meat relax.

Put the pan over a medium heat on top of the stove, sprinkle in the flour and mix to a smooth paste. Stir in the wine, red currant jelly, and ½ cup water. Season, bring to a boil, simmer for 3 minutes, then strain into a small pitcher. Carve the lamb and serve with the gravy.

With our fast pace of modern life, family roasts are all too infrequent, which is sad as we all love them. I remember Sunday roasts as a child with great warmth and affection. We would gather round the dinner table and Dad would carve the meat.

Everyone was at home—the kitchen gathering pace with pans simmering, pastry being made, drinks being poured, vegetables peeled, herbs chopped, and merry chatter and laughter. It's such a great and easy meal and all the family can be involved in preparation—children laying the table, gathering fruits or vegetables from the garden, helping in the kitchen, my mother making stuffings and sauces, and always my Dad pouring the drinks, choosing the wine, and for some reason he always washed the dishes.

It's that special meal when everyone can sit around the table and share good stories from the past week and talk about exciting forthcoming projects.

Children usually love eating a roast as there are so many elements to it—delicious roasted meat, vegetables in abundance, prepared in different ways, as well as sauces and gravy.

Then there is always the thrill and anticipation of the dessert—perhaps a pie served with lashings of cream, custard, or ice cream. Finally, for the adults, a small cup of coffee finishes off a fanatastic and succesful meal.

Next time you plan a Sunday roast pull out all the stops—create a happy feast and bring back good, strong, family traditions to your house. Just smell the food and listen to the laughter.

Roasted vegetables

All root vegetables are delicious roasted, but if there is something that you do not particularly like in this recipe, just omit it and replace with a family favorite.

The peeling of vegetables is a personal choice. Nutritionally, it is much better not to as many vitamins are stored just below the skin. Not peeling vegetables also saves time. However, unless your carrots are organically grown, it is essential to peel them.

3 tablespoons olive oil
4 medium potatoes, cut into chunks
4 small onions, halved with roots left intact
4 beets, halved
4 carrots, cut into chunks
4 parsnips, cut into chunks
sea salt and freshly ground black pepper

a roasting pan
Serves 4

Pour the oil into the roasting pan and put in a preheated oven at 400°F to heat.

If the vegetables are wet, pat them dry with paper towels.

Remove the pan of hot oil from the oven and add the potatoes, onions, and beets. Shake the pan until all the vegetables are coated with oil, then return to the oven and cook for 20 minutes.

Add the carrots and parsnips to the roasting pan and move all the vegetables around to ensure even cooking and coloring. Return to the oven to cook for a further 00 minutes.

Sprinkle with sea salt and freshly ground pepper and serve with the lamb.

Minted beans and peas

Mint sauce is a traditional accompaniment for roasted lamb, but I haven't included it in this menu because the rosemary will have already flavored the meat. Instead I am using mint with its other natural companion, peas, as well as delicious beans.

¾ cup sugar snap peas
¾ cup shelled fava beans or green beans
¾ cup sliced runner beans
¾ cup shelled peas, fresh or frozen
leaves from a bunch of mint, chopped
1½ tablespoons butter
sea salt and freshly ground black pepper

Serves 4

Bring a large saucepan of water to a boil. Add the peas and beans all at once, return to a boil, and simmer for 3 minutes.

Drain, then return the peas and beans to the pan. Add the mint, butter, salt, and pepper. Toss well and serve immediately.

Creamy mustard mash

Mashed potato with mustard is for me true comfort food on a fall or winter day. For a change, try adding a mixture of grated cheese, chopped herbs, and chopped scallions or fried onions. To give the potatoes a spicy kick, stir in finely chopped red chiles and a drizzle of chile oil.

3 lb. potatoes, cut into large cubes
⅔ cup milk
3 tablespoons olive oil
4 tablespoons butter
1 tablespoon powdered English mustard
sea salt and freshly ground black pepper

Serves 4

Put the potatoes in a saucepan of water, bring to a boil, then lower the heat and simmer for 20 minutes or until tender.

Drain the cooked potatoes thoroughly, then return them to the pan and set it over a low heat. Shake the pan and let the potatoes steam dry.

Put the milk, olive oil, and butter in a separate saucepan and warm gently.

Mash the potatoes well, being sure to crush out all the lumps. Alternatively, press the potatoes through a potato ricer.

Add the warm milk mixture, mustard, salt, and pepper to the mashed potatoes. Using a wooden spoon, beat well until smooth and well blended. Taste and adjust the seasoning.

top tip: Never try to mash potatoes in a food processor or blender, it will make them gluey. If cooking the mashed potatoes a little in advance of serving, cover them with some buttered waxed paper and keep them warm.

Braised red cabbage

This deliciously fruity winter vegetable dish can be made in advance and reheated—it actually improves with time and a second cooking. It is good served with most roasted meats and is a favorite component of the Scandinavian Christmas Eve meal of roasted pork, goose, or duck.

2 tablespoons butter
1 onion, chopped
1½ lb. red cabbage, cored and finely sliced
2 baking apples, cored, peeled, and chopped
¾ cup golden raisins
2 tablespoons brown sugar
2 tablespoons white wine vinegar
sea salt and freshly ground black pepper

Serves 4

Melt the butter in a large saucepan. Add the onion and cook over a low heat until softened.

Add the cabbage, apples, golden raisins, sugar, vinegar, and ¾ cup water. Season thoroughly and mix well.

Cover with a lid, bring to a boil, then simmer for 1 hour over a low heat. Check the cabbage occasionally, adding more water if needed.

Remove the lid and cook uncovered for a further 15 minutes. Adjust the seasoning, then serve hot.

top tip: For a festive flavor, add a couple of whole cloves, a bay leaf, a strip of orange peel, and some red wine at the same time as the cabbage.

Good old-fashioned desserts never really go out of fashion and are tops when it comes to cozy Sunday lunches with the family. Take a tip from grandma and keep portions on the generous side of large.

Chocolate pudding cake with raspberries

"Simple, pure indulgence" could be another name for this delicious and versatile dessert. If you prefer, it can be made the day before and stored in the fridge, then served at room temperature. Consider also putting it on the menu for dinner parties or afternoon tea.

8 oz. good-quality bitter chocolate, chopped
¾ cup (1½ sticks) plus 2 tablespoons butter
1 teaspoon instant coffee granules, dissolved in 1 tablespoon hot water
5 eggs
½ cup sugar
½ cup all-purpose flour
1 cup raspberries, about 6 oz.
confectioners' sugar or unsweetened cocoa, for dusting
¾ cup light cream, to serve

a 9-inch springform cake pan, greased and lined with waxed paper
Serves 4–6

Put the chopped chocolate, butter, and instant coffee mixture in a saucepan over a very low heat and stir until smooth and lump-free. Remove from the heat, set aside, and let cool.

Crack the eggs into a mixing bowl, add the sugar, and beat with an electric beater until light and fluffy, about 5 minutes.

Add the flour and chocolate mixture to the fluffy eggs and use a large metal spoon to fold them together until smooth.

Pour the batter into the prepared cake pan, sprinkle with the raspberries, and bake in a preheated oven at 325°F for 40 minutes or until the cake is firm to the touch and has come away from the sides of the pan.

Dust with confectioners' sugar or cocoa and serve with cream.

Lemon meringue pie

This lovely traditional dessert may seem complicated, but believe me it's worth it—the combination is heavenly and once you've made it, I think you'll cook it all the time. Don't ever skimp on the meringue, it has to be piled high to have the wow-factor. Try replacing the lemon with lime or orange and, for special occasions, try making this recipe into small individual tarts.

1⅔ cups all-purpose flour, plus extra for dusting
½ cup (1 stick) plus 1 tablespoon butter, cut into small pieces
2½ tablespoons sugar
2 egg yolks

Lemon filling
grated zest and juice of 3 lemons
⅔ cup sugar
4 tablespoons butter
¼ cup cornstarch
3 egg yolks

Meringue
3 egg whites
¾ cup plus 2 tablespoons sugar

an 8-inch false-bottom tart pan
waxed paper and baking beans or uncooked rice
Serves 4–6

To make the pastry, sift the flour into a bowl, then rub in the butter with your fingertips until it resembles fine breadcrumbs. Stir in the sugar.

Add the egg yolks and, using a round-bladed knife, cut through the mixture until the pastry starts to clump together. Knead briefly to ensure even mixing, then cover with plastic wrap and chill for 10 minutes.

Lightly dust a work surface with flour, then roll out the pastry and use it to line the tart pan. Cover and chill for 30 minutes.

Gently prick the base of the tart shell with a fork, then line with waxed paper and fill with baking beans or uncooked rice. Cook in a preheated oven at 375°F for 15 minutes.

Remove the tart shell from the oven and reduce the heat to 325°F. Lift the waxed paper and beans or rice out of the tart shell and return the shell to the oven for a further 5–10 minutes to dry out a little.

Meanwhile, to make the filling, put the lemon zest and juice into a small saucepan, then add the sugar, butter, and cornstarch. Stir, then gently heat to simmering point. When the mixture is thick, remove it from the heat and let cool for 5 minutes.

Beat the egg yolks into the filling and spoon into the cooked tart shell.

To make the meringue, beat the egg whites with an electric beater until stiff and standing in peaks. Add half the sugar and beat well, then quickly beat in the remaining sugar.

Pile the meringue on top of the lemon filling. Spread it evenly over the top and seal the meringue to the edge of the tart shell.

Cook in a preheated oven at 325°F for 15 minutes until the meringue is lightly golden. Serve hot (great) or cold (irresistible).

working lunch

In most people's working lives, every minute counts, but health must also be a priority. Remember that what we eat can make us feel good and work more efficiently. Try making your own lunch to take to work. When using these recipes, everyone will watch you enviously as you calmly sit at your desk and unwrap each day's delight.

Gazpacho

This soup tastes wonderful but is also very nutritious thanks to all the vitamin-rich raw ingredients. On a less healthy note, it also makes a terrific base for a totally delicious Bloody Mary!

1 onion, chopped
2 slices white bread, crusts removed
2 red bell peppers, seeded and diced
6 inches cucumber, peeled
1 garlic clove, crushed and chopped
4 celery stalks, diced
2¾ cups tomato passata
3 tablespoons olive oil
½ tablespoon white wine vinegar
a dash of Tabasco sauce
sea salt and freshly ground black pepper

Serves 4

Put the onion in a blender and work to a fine dice. Tear or dice the bread into pieces and add to the blender with the peppers, cucumber, garlic, and celery. Blend until finely chopped.

Add the passata, olive oil, vinegar, Tabasco, salt, and pepper to the blender, add 1¼ cups water, and blend for 3 minutes.

Chill the soup overnight until very cold, then transfer to a thermos flask and keep in the fridge until ready to serve.

Cheese-stuffed croissants

A great portable snack, best made with your favorite cheese—I like Gruyère or brie. This is the classic recipe, but you can use sliced tomatoes or lightly cooked sliced mushrooms instead of the ham.

4 croissants
2 teaspoons Dijon mustard
4 slices cheese
4 thick slices Black Forest smoked ham
freshly ground black pepper

a baking tray
Serves 4

Cut the croissants in half lengthwise and open out. Spread each croissant with ½ teaspoon Dijon mustard, then add the cheese, ham, and pepper.

Transfer to a baking tray and cook in a preheated oven at 350°F for 10 minutes. Serve hot or cold.

Salad box

Simple to make and flexible, this lunch box
includes whatever things are in your fridge.

1 eggplant, sliced lengthwise
4 zucchini, sliced lengthwise
2 cups canned lima beans, 15 oz., rinsed and
 drained
2 cups cooked penne pasta
4 tomatoes, sliced
4 hard-cooked eggs, peeled and halved
a bunch of flat-leaf parsley, chopped
¼ cup caperberries, or 4 teaspoons capers,
¼ cup olive oil
2 tablespoons balsamic vinegar
4 oz. Parmesan cheese, shaved with a peeler
1 lemon, quartered lengthwise
sea salt and freshly ground black pepper

Serves 4

Cook the eggplant and zucchini on a stove-top
grill pan over medium heat for about
4–5 minutes on each side.

Divide the beans and pasta between 4 lunch
boxes. Add the eggplant, zucchini, tomatoes,
boiled eggs, parsley, and caperberries or capers.
Mix well.

Sprinkle the salads with the olive oil and
balsamic vinegar. Season with salt and pepper
and top with shavings of Parmesan.

Add a wedge of lemon to each box, cover with
the lids, and chill overnight. Take to work and eat
at room temperature.

Chicken salad wrap

4 soft flour tortillas, preferably whole-wheat
4 tablespoons mayonnaise
2 teaspoons whole-grain mustard
2 cooked chicken breasts, shredded
2 carrots, grated
a wedge of white cabbage, finely sliced
2 medium tomatoes, finely sliced
sea salt and freshly ground black pepper

Serves 4

Lay each tortilla flat on a piece of waxed paper. Spread with the mayonnaise and mustard.

Add the shredded chicken, grated carrot, sliced cabbage, salt, pepper, and tomato.

Roll up the tortillas into tight cylinders, using the waxed paper to help you. Twist the ends of the paper together.

Cut the cylinders in half diagonally. Wrap each portion in plastic and chill until ready for work.

top tip: If you want to make your own lunches, a clever trick is to keep it in mind the night before when you are cooking dinner. Any extra chicken, meats, fish, boiled eggs, potatoes, pasta, rice, or roasted vegetables such as pumpkin, bell peppers, or onions can be used in a wonderful sandwich or salad.

Chicken and vegetable satay sticks with noodle salad

Satays look spectacular, so this is a perfect lunch to serve at meetings. It also caters for any vegetarians that may be in the group. Soaking the satay sticks is important—it prevents them burning under the broiler.

2 chicken breasts
1 eggplant, cut into 8 chunks
8 mushrooms
2 zucchini, cut into 8 chunks
1 red or yellow bell pepper, cut into 8 chunks
¾ cup soy sauce
3 tablespoons smooth peanut butter
2 tablespoons vegetable oil
1 onion, sliced
1 garlic clove, crushed and chopped
1 inch fresh ginger, peeled and sliced
4 oz. beanthread noodles
⅔ cup chopped peanuts
a bunch of cilantro leaves

16 wooden satay sticks, soaked in water for at
    least 30 minutes
a baking tray, lightly oiled
Serves 4

Cut each chicken breast into 4 strips, then thread onto 8 of the soaked satay sticks.

Thread the eggplant, mushrooms, zucchini, and bell pepper alternately onto another 8 sticks.

In a bowl or pitcher, mix ½ cup of the soy sauce with the peanut butter and ¼ cup water. Use this mixture to baste the satay sticks all over.

Arrange the sticks on the oiled baking tray and cook under a preheated broiler for 12 minutes, turning occasionally to brown evenly.

Heat the oil in a wok or skillet. Add the onion, garlic, and ginger and stir-fry over a medium heat without browning.

Meanwhile, bring a large saucepan of water to a boil. Add the noodles, boil for 1 minute, then drain immediately.

Add the noodles to the wok or skillet, then the peanuts, cilantro, and remaining soy sauce. Stir well to mix.

Divide the mixture between 4 lunch boxes and top with the cooked satay sticks. Let cool, then chill overnight. If you're taking this to work, store the boxes in the office fridge and remove them 20 minutes before serving.

To help fit everything into your day, have some informal meetings round a conference table laid out with a delicious but easy-to-eat lunch. That's delicious time management...

food on the move

This is a very modern way of eating. Since we all lack time, we have to utilize it cleverly, so sitting on a train or taking a walk while snacking is increasingly common. But food taken on the hoof can be a treat—take inspiration from these recipes and enjoy the freedom.

Tomato and goat cheese tart

Oh, how I love this tart—the crumbly, flaky texture of the puff pastry, the finely sliced onions and roasted tomatoes, then melted goat cheese binding them altogether. Puff pastry can be bought frozen or from the chiller cabinets. It even comes pre-rolled for the super-busy person. I think it's always worth having a package in the freezer as it is very versatile and can be quickly made into savory or sweet tarts.

13 oz. ready-made puff pastry
2 onions, finely sliced
8 oz. roasted baby tomatoes (page 69)
6 oz. soft, rindless goat cheese, crumbled
2 tablespoons olive oil
1 teaspoon sugar
sea salt and freshly ground black pepper

a saucer, 6 inches diameter
a baking tray, lightly oiled
Serves 4

Roll out the pastry and cut 4 circles using the saucer as a template. Transfer to the baking tray. Prick the pastry all over with a fork.

Bake in a preheated oven at 375°F for 15 minutes, then remove from the oven, but leave the oven at the same temperature.

Put the sliced onion in a bowl with the tomatoes, goat cheese, olive oil, sugar, salt, and pepper and mix well. Divide the mixture between the pastry bases, spreading it evenly over the top and pushing down gently.

Return the tarts to the oven and cook for 20 minutes, then reduce the heat to 350°F and cook for a further 15–20 minutes until lightly browned. Serve hot or at room temperature.

Steak and tomato sandwich

Such a classic sandwich and really very delicious! Always use very fresh bread—I think bread made with unbleached flour is best

olive oil, for greasing
4 sirloin steaks, 3 oz. each
8 slices bread
butter, for spreading
4 teaspoons Dijon mustard
2 large ripe tomatoes, sliced
2 packages arugula, about 4 oz.
sea salt and freshly ground black pepper

Serves 4

Heat a stove-top grill pan or a nonstick skillet with a little olive oil. When very hot, add the steaks and cook 1 minute on each side for rare steak, 2 minutes each side for medium, or 3 minutes each side for well done.

Meanwhile, spread 4 slices of the bread with butter and mustard, then add the sliced tomatoes and arugula.

Top with the cooked steak and sprinkle with salt and pepper. Butter the remaining slices of bread and put them on top of the steaks. Press together, wrap in a napkin, and eat as you walk out of the house.

Hummus and salad in Turkish flatbread

If Turkish flatbread is hard to find, use pita bread instead—just toast it lightly, open up the pocket, and fill with all the ingredients given here.

4 sheets very thin Turkish flatbread
¾ cup hummus
¼ head iceberg lettuce
2 avocados, halved, pitted, and sliced
juice of 1 lemon
2 tablespoons olive oil
sea salt and freshly ground black pepper

Serves 4

Open out the flatbreads and lay each one on a piece of waxed paper. Spread evenly with the hummus.

Shred the iceberg lettuce finely and scatter it over the bread. Arrange the sliced avocado on top, then sprinkle with the lemon juice and olive oil. Season generously with salt and pepper.

With the help of the waxed paper, roll up the bread and filling tightly and shape with your hands into a cylinder, twisting the paper at each end.

Cut the cylinders in half, then wrap in a napkin and go. Eat the wraps within 3 hours of making for a really good, fresh taste.

Focaccia with broiled chicken

This sandwich is a meal in itself: wrap it in plastic and eat on long journeys. Choose buffalo milk mozzarella whenever possible—it tastes indisputably better than cows' milk.

2 chicken fillets, halved lengthwise
1 loaf focaccia bread
1 garlic clove, halved lengthwise
2 tomatoes, sliced
5 oz. mozzarella cheese, sliced
a large bunch of basil, leaves torn
2 tablespoons olive oil
sea salt and freshly ground black pepper
Serves 4

Cook the chicken on a preheated grill pan or under a broiler for 5–6 minutes on each side, or until cooked right through. Remove and set aside.

Cut the focaccia in half lengthwise and put the bread cut-side down on the grill pan or cut-side up under the broiler. Cook until lightly toasted.

Remove the bread from the heat and rub the toasted surface with the garlic clove.

Put a piece of focaccia, toasted-side up, on a board. Top with the chicken, tomatoes, cheese, basil, olive oil, salt, and pepper.

Cover with a second piece of focaccia and press down. Repeat with the remaining ingredients.

Cut into portions, wrap in plastic or cellophane, and put in bags or boxes for transportation.

Ham and thyme tortilla

The Spaniards serve tortilla (omelet) as a tapas snack. It is delicious cold too, so makes the ideal meal for people on the go.

3 medium potatoes
3 tablespoons olive oil
2 onions, sliced
4 oz. ham, chopped
5 eggs
¼ cup milk
leaves from 8 sprigs of thyme, coarsely chopped
¾ cup grated Gruyère cheese
sea salt and freshly ground black pepper

an ovenproof skillet
Serves 4–6

Cook the potatoes in boiling water until just tender. Drain and cool, then slice.

Heat the olive oil in a medium skillet. Add the onions and cook over a moderate heat for 7 minutes or until soft and lightly golden. Add the ham and potatoes and mix thoroughly.

Beat the eggs in a bowl, then add the milk, thyme, and some salt and pepper. Pour into the skillet and mix carefully.

Sprinkle with the cheese and cook over a medium heat for 8 minutes. Reduce the heat and cook for another 10 minutes, until the egg has almost set.

Put the skillet under a preheated broiler and cook until the cheese is golden and bubbling.

Remove from the heat. Check that the tortilla is firm, then invert it onto a plate. Place another plate on top and turn the tortilla over again to reveal the golden cheese topping. Serve.

The secret of good food on the move is practical packaging. Keep a selection of sturdy boxes, waxed paper, cellophane bags, and cloth or paper napkins ready to wrap your snack foods. Some things, such as the tortilla, travel better whole, so take it in the skillet and carry a small knife with you to cut it into wedges when hungry.

snack attack

We all get the munchies, but next time, instead of reaching for that package of chips or bar of chocolate, make a little effort and try preparing one of these snacks. Pure, fresh, and nutritious foods, they will stop all rumblings in your tummy and taste good too.

Zucchini and Cheddar on toast

Here is a simple combination that tastes like heaven—just make sure that you squeeze the grated zucchini well.

2 zucchini, grated
1⅔ cups freshly grated mature Cheddar or
  Monterey Jack cheese
1 shallot, finely diced
1 small egg
a dash of Worcestershire sauce
4 slices bread, toasted
sea salt and freshly ground black pepper

a baking tray
Serves 4

Put the grated zucchini in a clean, dry dish cloth and twist tightly, squeezing out excess liquid.

Transfer to a mixing bowl and add the cheese, shallot, egg, Worcestershire sauce, salt, and pepper. Stir thoroughly.

Put the toasted bread onto the baking tray, pile the zucchini mixture on top, and cook under a preheated broiler until golden brown. Serve hot.

Banana smoothie

To me, this is bliss in the summer and it quickly rids me of any hunger pangs.

4 large, ripe bananas
2 cups cold milk
1 cup ice
2 tablespoons honey
1 tablespoon rolled oats
1 tablespoon bran
Serves 4

Chop the bananas into a blender. Add all the remaining ingredients and blend until smooth. Serve in large glasses and taste the goodness.

Mountain eggs

I first came across this dish in the Swiss Alps where they cook and serve it in small, individual skillets. Whenever hunger struck us between meals, we rushed straight into a little restaurant for a skillet of these eggs. Ham is traditional, but this is also very good with chorizo sausage. If you are vegetarian, replace the ham with mushrooms.

4 teaspoons olive oil
4 large cooked potatoes, sliced 1 inch thick
1½ cups (8 oz.) smoked ham, chopped
4 eggs
4 slices Emmental cheese, ½ inch thick, or 1 cup grated Emmental
sea salt and freshly ground black pepper
chopped flat-leaf parsley, to serve (optional)

Serves 4

Heat 1 teaspoon of oil in each of 4 small skillets. Add the potatoes and cook for 2 minutes on each side. Stir in the ham.

Crack an egg into each pan. Top with the sliced or grated cheese, sprinkle with salt and pepper, and cook for 2–3 minutes until the egg is just set and the cheese is beginning to melt.

Serve sprinkled with chopped parsley, if using.

Blue cheese and tomato crostini

Here is a fantastic snack to enjoy while relaxing with a glass of wine or beer and some friends. If you don't like blue cheese, Italian mozzarella, Taleggio, or soft goat cheeses are good alternatives.

4 slices sourdough bread or 8 slices baguette
1 garlic clove
2 tablespoons olive oil
4 oz. blue cheese
2 tomatoes, sliced
sea salt and freshly ground black pepper

Serves 4

Toast the bread slices on each side. Rub them with the garlic, using them like a grater, then sprinkle each slice with ½ tablespoon olive oil.

Crumble half the blue cheese with your fingers and divide it between the 4 slices of toast.

Top with the sliced tomatoes, in single layer, then cover with the remaining cheese. Sprinkle lightly with salt and pepper.

Cook the crostini under a preheated broiler set to high, until the cheese begins to brown lightly, about 4-5 minutes. Serve hot or warm.

Afternoon tea is such a pretty meal, so go for it! Dig out that beautiful floral china your grandmother gave you, shake an embroidered cloth over the table, and get baking. When your friends arrive at 4 pm, pour steaming cups of tea, spread biscuits with strawberry jelly, and giggle the hours away—what fun!

teatime

Sodabread

Country people work hard and the traditional way to top up their energy levels is with a substantial meal at teatime. Served with a good flavorful Cheddar or Monterey Jack, this lovely bread provides the perfect boost.

3 1/3 cups whole-wheat flour
1 teaspoon baking soda
1 teaspoon cream of tartar
a pinch of salt
2 tablespoons butter, cut into small cubes
1 1/4 cups milk

a baking tray, lightly floured
Makes 1 loaf

Sift the flour, baking soda, cream of tartar, and salt into a large bowl. Rub the butter into the flour with your fingertips.

Make a well in the center. Pour in the milk and mix with a round-bladed knife to give a soft dough.

Turn out the dough onto a lightly floured surface and knead until smooth, about 4 minutes. Shape the dough into a round loaf 6 inches diameter and flatten the top slightly.

Place on the baking tray and use a sharp knife to score a cross about 1/2 inch deep in the top of the dough, making quarters.

Bake in a preheated oven at 350°F for about 35 minutes. Remove from the oven and, protecting your hands with a dish cloth, tap the bottom of the loaf with your knuckles—when cooked, it should sound hollow; if it doesn't, bake for a few minutes more.

Serve warm, topped with slices of mature cheese or spread with butter and jelly.

top tip: Sandwiches are a must at teatime. Try making them with a variety of all the great breads that are available in the stores. Good combinations include sodabread with egg or tuna, walnut bread with Cheddar and finely sliced celery, sourdough with smoked ham, focaccia with smoked salmon and pepper, or ciabatta with mozzarella and basil.

Cucumber sandwiches with cream cheese

If you want to be truly traditional, remove the crusts with a serrated knife and cut each sandwich into 3 fingers before serving. When I make them, I leave the crusts on and cut the sandwiches into 4 fingers.

8 inches cucumber
8 slices mixed grain bread
butter, for spreading
1/2 cup cream cheese
sea salt and freshly ground black pepper
Serves 4

Peel and finely slice the cucumber.

Spread each slice of bread lightly with the butter. Take 4 slices and spread them with a layer of cream cheese. Sprinkle some salt and pepper over the top, then add a generous layer of the sliced cucumber.

Place a second slice of bread on top of each sandwich, carefully press together, then cut.

Egg and watercress rolls

Summer days and teatime on a rug in the garden with egg and cress rolls—happy memories of my childhood. It makes me smile and want to start boiling eggs! Tiny sprouted mustard and cress leaves are traditional, but watercress is also good.

3 hard-cooked eggs, peeled and chopped
1 tablespoon mayonnaise
4 soft bread rolls
butter, for spreading
leaves from a small bunch of watercress
sea salt and freshly ground black pepper
Makes 4

Put the eggs and mayonnaise in a bowl, season and mix well.

Cut the bread rolls in half lengthwise and lightly spread with butter. Fill with the egg mayonnaise and top with the watercress leaves. Close the rolls and serve.

Golden raisin biscuits

If friends turn up on your doorstep and catch you unprepared, biscuits are incredibly easy and speedy to make, and they're best eaten straight out of the oven. All you need then is butter and fruit jelly.

3⅓ cups self-rising flour
½ cup (1 stick) butter, cut into small pieces
⅔ cup golden raisins
1¼ cups milk, plus extra for glazing

a baking tray, lightly floured
a 2-inch cookie cutter, lightly floured
Makes 8

Sift the flour into a large mixing bowl, then rub in the butter with your fingertips until the mixture looks like fine breadcrumbs.

Stir the golden raisins into the flour mixture. Make a well in the center and pour in the milk. Mix with a round-bladed knife until the liquid is incorporated and the mixture is soft and spongy.

Turn out the dough onto a lightly floured work surface and knead it for 2–3 minutes until smooth.

Press or roll out the dough to 1 inch thick. Using the floured cookie cutter, cut out 6–8 rounds. Brush the tops of the biscuits with a little milk.

Put on the baking tray and cook in a preheated oven at 425°F for 10–12 minutes until well risen, frim to the touch, and lightly golden. Remove from the oven and eat hot or warm.

top tip: You can make many variations on this reliable biscuit recipe by using other fruit instead of the golden raisins. Don't restrict yourself to dried varieties—even fresh fruit such as finely chopped apple, apricots, bananas, or cherries work well. Choose a jelly to match for real pizzazz!

Lemon and ginger infusion

This delicious hot drink can also help to soothe a sore throat. If you want to give it a festive kick, add a dash of whiskey.

zest and juice of 3 lemons
2 inches fresh ginger, peeled and sliced
a bunch of mint leaves

To serve
1 inch fresh ginger, peeled and finely sliced
1 lemon, finely sliced
sugar or honey (optional)
Serves 4

Put the lemon zest and juice, ginger, and mint in a heatproof pitcher. Pour on 3 cups boiling water and leave the mixture to steep for 6 minutes.

Serve hot in teacups with slices of ginger and lemon. Sweeten to taste with sugar or honey.

Iced jasmine tea

Keep this refreshing and cooling drink in the fridge to sip throughout a hot summer's day.

2 teaspoons jasmine tea
ice cubes (see method)
2 peaches, pitted and sliced
1 lemon, sliced
Serves 4

Put the tea in a pitcher, add 3 cups boiling water, and brew for 5 minutes. Strain and let cool.

Half-fill a large glass pitcher with ice cubes, add the sliced peaches and lemon, then pour over the cooled tea and mix well. Serve immediately.

Strawberry tarts

I can't resist these very special tarts, and when the strawberry season is at its peak I make them often.

2 cups all-purpose flour
²⁄₃ cup (1¼ sticks) butter
¾ cup sugar
4 egg yolks
²⁄₃ cup redcurrant jelly
1 lb. strawberries, hulled but left whole

To serve
confectioners' sugar, for dusting
about 1 cup whipped cream

8 false-bottom tartlet pans, 4 inches diameter, greased
waxed paper and baking beans or uncooked rice
Makes 6–8

Put the flour in a large mixing bowl, then rub in the butter with your fingertips until the mixture looks like fine breadcrumbs.

Using a round-bladed knife, mix in the sugar, then the egg yolks until the dough forms a ball.

Turn out the dough onto a work surface lightly dusted with flour. Knead quickly until the dough

is smooth, then wrap it in plastic and put in the refrigerator for 20 minutes.

Put the chilled dough on a work surface lightly dusted with flour. Roll out to about ⅛ inch thick, then use to line the tartlet pans.

Prick the base of each tart shell a few times with a fork, then line with waxed paper and baking beans or rice. Bake in a preheated oven at 400°F for 15 minutes.

Remove the tartlet shells from the oven and remove the waxed paper and baking beans or rice. Return the shells to the oven for a further 5–10 minutes, until the pastry is set and light golden. Remove them from the oven and let cool in the pans.

Melt the redcurrant jelly in a small saucepan with 2 tablespoons water. When the tart shells are cool, brush the interiors with a little red currant glaze and let set (this stops the fruit juices making the pastry soggy).

Arrange the strawberries in the tart shells.

Add 1 tablespoon water to the glaze left in the saucepan and heat through. Brush or spoon the glaze over the fruit and let cool and set.

Remove the tarts from the pans, dust lightly with confectioners' sugar and serve with a little whipped cream.

Lemon syrup cake

This really is the simplest yet most delicious cake ever. In our house we can't even wait for it to cool before tucking in!

1 cup (2 sticks) butter
1¼ cups sugar
4 eggs
grated zest of 4 lemons
1⅔ cups self-rising flour

Lemon syrup
juice of 4 lemons
¾ cup sugar

a loaf pan, 9 x 5 x 3 inches, buttered
Makes 1 loaf

Cream the butter and sugar in a large mixing bowl until light and soft. Beat in the eggs one at a time. Using a metal spoon, carefully fold in the lemon zest and flour.

Place in the prepared pan and bake in a preheated oven at 400°F for 35 minutes.

Insert a knife or skewer in the middle of the cake—if it comes out clean, the cake is cooked. If not, return to the oven for another 5 minutes.

Remove the cake from the oven, let cool in the pan for 5 minutes, then turn out onto a plate.

To make the lemon syrup, put the lemon juice and sugar in a small saucepan and heat gently until the sugar has melted.

Spike the cake with a skewer and spoon the syrup over the top, allowing it to slowly sink in. Repeat until all the syrup has been used.

Celebration frosted fruitcake

Although this moist cake takes quite a long time to cook—3½ hours—it really is worth it to mark a family celebration.

2 cups raisins
2 cups currants
2 cups golden raisins
1 cup chopped mixed peel
½ cup undyed candied cherries
1½ cups (3 sticks) butter, melted
1½ cups raw sugar
4 eggs
2 cups all-purpose flour
2 teaspoons apple pie spice
½ teaspoon ground cinnamon
a pinch of nutmeg
3 tablespoons Madeira or sherry, plus extra
   for sprinkling (optional)

Frosting
2 tablespoons apricot jelly
confectioners' sugar, for dusting
1 lb. ready-to-roll marzipan
1 lb. ready-to-roll white frosting

a springform cake pan, 8 inches diameter,
   greased and lined with waxed paper
Makes 1 cake

Put the dried fruits, peel, and candied cherries in a large bowl and mix well. Add the melted butter, sugar, eggs, flour, apple pie spice, cinnamon, nutmeg, and the Madeira or sherry. Mix well.

Spoon the mixture into the prepared cake pan and bake on the middle rack of a preheated oven at 300°F. Cook for 3–3½ hours or until a skewer inserted in the center of the cake comes out clean.

When cooked, let the cake cool in the pan for 25 minutes, then remove from the pan and let cool completely on a wire rack.

If you like a really boozy, moist cake, drizzle with an extra spoonful of Madeira or sherry before wrapping the cake in paper. Store in an airtight container or wrapped in plastic for up to 3 weeks.

A few days before the celebration, frost the cake. Melt the apricot jelly with ½ tablespoon water, then brush on the top and sides of the cake.

Dust a work surface with confectioners' sugar, add the marzipan, and roll out to ⅛ inch thick. Measure the height and circumference of the cake, then cut a rectangular strip of marzipan to fit those measurements. Wrap it around the cake, pressing the join together to seal.

Using a plate or cake pan as a template, cut a circle of marzipan to fit the top of the cake exactly. Lay it over the top of the cake and smooth out with your hands. Use a pin to burst any air bubbles and gently press out the air with your fingers.

Brush the marzipan surface of the cake with water. Repeat the same process you used with the marzipan using the ready-to-roll frosting, making sure the surface is dusted with confectioners' sugar to prevent sticking. Using your fingers, carefully rub all the joins together (the more you rub, the more invisible they become).

Again, prick any air holes with a pin and press out the air. Decorate immediately or store the cake in an airtight container until needed. I like my cake plain and simple and decorated with a few buds or petals and maybe a beautiful gauze ribbon tied around the side.

top tip: To make a special gift for someone, wrap the cake in cellophane and tie it with a big bow. Write a personalized message on a tag and attach it to the gift. This is delightful.

Coconut jelly cookies

1 cup sugar
¾ cup (1⅔ sticks) butter, softened
1⅔ cups unsweetened shredded coconut
2 eggs
1⅓ cups all-purpose flour
1 jar fruit jelly, about 12 oz.

a baking tray, lined with waxed paper
Makes 12

Put the sugar and butter in a bowl and using a wooden spoon or electric beater, cream the mixture until light and fluffy.

Add the coconut and eggs, mix well, then sift in the flour and stir until smooth.

Put teaspoons of the mixture spaced well apart onto the prepared baking sheet—don't set them too close to each other as they need room to spread while in the oven.

Bake in a preheated oven at 250°F for about 10–12 minutes until lightly golden.

Remove from the oven and let cool and set for 5 minutes on the tray. Then remove to a wire rack to cool completely.

Repeat until all the cookie mixture is used, making at least 24 cookies.

When cool, spread the flat side of each one with ½ teaspoon jelly and sandwich together. Store in an airtight container and eat quickly.

top tip: To vary these cookies, sandwich them together with other fillings. Try a different fruit jelly, some lemon or other citrus curd, sweetened prune purée, or decadent cream cheese frosting mixed with candied peel.

night

The more life rushes by, the more I think it is important to make a good meal in the evening, pour a glass of wine or shake a cocktail, lay a table or tray, and then laugh the day away with family or friends. No matter how hectic the day has been, it is possible to prepare a good home-cooked meal at night. There are plenty of ideas in this chapter for one-pot and one-bowl meals to eat informally, but even the party food and romantic dinners featured here can be quickly rustled up. For special occasions, it is fun to make a little fuss and throw an extravagant party. I enjoy planning the perfect menu and setting the scene with flowers, twinkling candles, and my favorite tableware. After the feast, serve rich chocolates with fresh, steaming-hot coffee in small glasses (very cosmopolitan) and chat away with your friends until the early hours—what a delightful way to end the day and start tomorrow.

weekday meals pantry basics dinner on a tray comfort food one-pot meals elegant drinks and finger food party time dinner for friends twilight barbecue dinner party dream dinner date late night feast

weekday meals

This is what I call "Formula-One cooking"—fast, furious, and delivering a podium-stand winner for supper. It's so simple. From spinach salad with bacon dressing to a quick Thai noodle salad via lemon spaghetti oozing with fresh citrus flavors. If these win in your house, why not pop open the champagne and take a bow?

Spinach and bacon salad with Dijon dressing

8 oz. young spinach leaves, trimmed, washed, and dried in a salad spinner, about 2 cups
4 hard-cooked eggs, peeled and quartered
12 cherry tomatoes, halved
12 slices of bacon, broiled, then chopped
2 avocados, halved, pitted, and chopped
whole-wheat bread, to serve

Dijon dressing
juice of 1 lemon
1 tablespoon white wine vinegar
1 teaspoon Dijon mustard
¼ cup sunflower or vegetable oil
1 teaspoon sugar
sea salt and freshly ground black pepper
Serves 4

Put the spinach in a bowl. Add the quartered eggs, cherry tomatoes, bacon, and avocados.

To make the dressing, mix the lemon juice, vinegar, and mustard together in a bowl, then slowly beat in the oil.

Stir the sugar and some salt and pepper into the dressing. Mix well, pour over the salad, and serve with chunks of whole-wheat bread.

top tip: For perfect hard-cooked eggs, cook them in simmering water for about 9 minutes, then drain and run under cold water until the eggs are quite cold. To peel, gently tap the eggs on a flat, hard surface to crack the shells all over, then peel under running water. If eggs are very fresh the shell won't come away easily from the white—so, if the peeled egg looks messy, at least you know it was fresh.

Lemon spaghetti
This is a favorite meal in our house—it's delicious and very quick to make. If more sustenance is needed, broil some fish such as halibut or skate and serve on top.

10 oz. dried spaghetti
1 garlic clove, chopped
grated zest and juice of 2 lemons
¼ cup olive oil
1 cup freshly grated Parmesan cheese
a bunch of flat-leaf parsley, coarsely chopped
sea salt and freshly ground black pepper
Serves 4

Bring a saucepan of water to a boil, add the spaghetti, stir, and cook for about 9 minutes.

Put the garlic in a bowl and mix in the lemon zest, juice, and oil.

Drain the pasta well, then return to the pan, add the lemon mixture, Parmesan, parsley, salt, and pepper. Toss well and serve immediately.

Thai noodle salad

Shrimp powder is sold in plastic sachets or jars in Chinese stores and other Asian markets. It is made from shredded, dried miniature shrimp. Like fish sauce, it acts as a general seasoning. If you can't find it, use extra fish sauce or even soy sauce.

4 oz. cellophane noodles
1 tablespoon peanut or sunflower oil
1 white onion, diced
1 inch fresh ginger, peeled and diced
1 red chile, seeded and diced
1 garlic clove, crushed and chopped
¼ cup ground pork
2 oz. shelled shrimp, finely chopped
6 scallions, sliced
a bunch of cilantro, chopped
1 teaspoon fish sauce
1 teaspoon shrimp powder
2 limes, one juiced and the other cut
    into wedges

Serves 4

Soak the cellophane noodles in a bowl of cold water for 10 minutes until soft. Drain well.

Meanwhile, heat the oil in a wok. Add the onion, ginger, chile, and garlic and stir-fry over a medium heat for 5 minutes.

Add the pork and cook for 5 minutes, stirring well to break it up. Add the shrimp and cook for 3 minutes, then remove from the heat.

Add the scallions, cilantro, fish sauce, shrimp powder, lime juice, and drained noodles. Toss well and serve with the lime wedges.

top tip: Try cooked chicken instead of pork and shrimp.

Couscous with roasted chicken and vegetables

Remember that your freezer can be a convenient source of good food. Most people don't really use theirs, except for ice cubes, ice cream, schnapps, and the odd package of frozen peas or chicken pieces, but that's what's needed for this great meal.

8 small chicken pieces, thawed if frozen, and excess fat removed
2 onions, cut into wedges
4 garlic cloves
1 eggplant, cut into chunks
2 zucchini, sliced
1 cup frozen peas
leaves from a bunch of flat-leaf parsley, chopped
⅔ cup couscous
a pinch of saffron threads
olive oil, for roasting (see method)
sea salt and freshly ground black pepper

a heavy-bottom roasting pan, lightly oiled
Serves 4

Arrange the chicken pieces in the roasting pan. Cook in a preheated oven at 375°F for 10 minutes.

Remove the chicken to a plate and set aside. Add the onions, garlic, and eggplant to the pan and toss them in the cooking juices, drizzling with a little oil if necessary.

Add the chicken pieces to the pan. Roast for a further 30 minutes, turning after 15 minutes to ensure even browning. Add the zucchini, peas, and parsley to the roasting pan for the final 8 minutes of cooking.

Pour 1¼ cups boiling water into a saucepan and put over a high heat. Add the couscous and saffron and simmer for 5 minutes. Drain thoroughly, transfer to a large serving dish, season with salt and pepper, and fluff up with a fork.

Arrange the cooked chicken and vegetables on top of the couscous, cover, and keep warm.

Use a metal spoon to skim off any excess fat from the roasting pan. Put the pan on the stove and heat to simmering. Add ⅔ cup water, salt, and pepper and boil for 4 minutes. Pour over the chicken and couscous and serve.

pantry basics

Some weeks seem to whizz by with no time for a shopping trip, but don't fear: it's amazing what great meals can be made from pantry staples. Make sure you keep stocked up on essentials such as onions, garlic, olive oil, Parmesan, dried mushrooms, cans of chopped tomatoes and beans, dried pasta and noodles, plus risotto, brown, and long-grain rice. Then you'll always be able to prepare a delicious and nutritious dinner for the family or unexpected visitors.

Spaghetti puttanesca

A simple and stylish pasta dish to cook at home, this traditional Italian recipe never seems to lose its appeal. Whenever I find a new Mediterranean gourmet store, I look for special pantry items. Anchovies, either in oil or salted, are very good, as are the jars of tiny capers. Both ingredients are real gems that make this piquant pantry dish just as memorable as it can be when eaten on holiday.

10 oz. dried spaghetti
4 tomatoes, peeled, seeded, and chopped
1 cup pitted black olives
3 oz. canned anchovies, chopped
3 tablespoons capers
leaves from a large bunch of flat-leaf parsley, chopped
¼ cup olive oil
freshly ground black pepper
¾ cup freshly grated Parmesan cheese, to serve
Serves 4

Bring a large saucepan of water to a boil, then add the dried spaghetti, stir well to separate the strands, and simmer for 9 minutes.

When the spaghetti is cooked, drain thoroughly. Dry the saucepan, then return the spaghetti to the pan and add the tomatoes, olives, anchovies, capers, parsley, and olive oil. Sprinkle with pepper.

Toss the pasta well and serve with a dish of freshly grated Parmesan for sprinkling.

Spaghetti bolognese

To me, spaghetti bolognese should contain lots of rich tomato sauce and just a little meat. It requires slow simmering to blend all the flavors and make a thick sauce to coat the spaghetti. Children and adults love this recipe. Instead of Parmesan, try serving it with some coarsely grated mature Cheddar cheese, which is my favorite.

¼ cup olive oil
2 onions, diced
2 garlic cloves, crushed and finely chopped
1 teaspoon dried mixed herbs
1 cup good-quality ground beef
3 cups canned chopped tomatoes
2 tablespoons tomato purée
10 oz. dried spaghetti
sea salt and freshly ground black pepper
1 cup grated fresh Parmesan or mature
  Cheddar cheese, to serve
Serves 4

Heat the olive oil in a large saucepan. Add the onions and cook for 5 minutes over a medium heat until softened but not browned. Add the garlic and cook for a further 1 minute.

Stir in the dried mixed herbs and ground beef, stirring thoroughly with a large spoon to break up the beef. Cook for 5 minutes.

Stir in the chopped tomatoes, tomato purée, salt, and pepper. Bring the mixture to a boil, then lower the heat and simmer for 45 minutes, stirring occasionally. Check the consistency of the sauce from time to time and add a little water if needed. When cooked, the sauce should be a rich, deep red and thickly coat the back of a spoon.

Bring a large saucepan of water to a boil. Add the spaghetti, stir well to separate the strands, and simmer for 9 minutes.

Drain the pasta well and divide between 4 deep serving bowls. Top with the sauce, sprinkle with grated cheese, and serve hot.

Classic tomato sauce for pasta

Every cook should be able to make this classic tomato sauce. It's not only good with pasta, but great with broiled fish, and can be added to meat casseroles to give extra richness, or spiced up with harissa to make a sauce for vegetables and couscous.

¼ cup olive oil, plus extra for drizzling
2 onions, chopped
2 garlic cloves, crushed and chopped
4½ cups canned chopped tomatoes
2 teaspoons dried mixed herbs
a pinch of crushed dried chiles
1 lb. dried spaghetti or penne pasta
sea salt and freshly ground black pepper
1 cup grated fresh Parmesan or mature
   Cheddar cheese, to serve

Serves 4

Heat the olive oil in a medium saucepan. Add the onion and garlic and cook for 4 minutes over a medium heat until softened but not browned.

Stir in the chopped tomatoes, mixed herbs, dried chiles, salt, and pepper. Simmer over a low heat for 25 minutes, stirring occasionally, until the sauce thickens and intensifies in flavor.

Bring a large saucepan of water to a boil, add the pasta, and cook for 9 minutes. Drain well, then toss with 1 tablespoon olive oil.

Add the sauce to the pasta and mix through. Sprinkle with the grated cheese and serve hot.

top tip: You can vary this sauce by including some chopped capers, olives, fresh herbs (torn basil, chopped rosemary, marjoram, thyme, chives, parsley, or sorrel), grated zucchini, chopped crispy bacon, crumbled goat cheese, or mozzarella—all added just for the last few minutes of cooking.

Curried lentils and spinach

Forget any lentil dishes you may not have enjoyed in the past—this is just so delicious, all the flavors bring the lentils to life.

¼ cup olive oil
1 onion, diced
1 garlic clove, chopped
1 teaspoon ground cumin or garam masala
1 teaspoon medium hot curry powder
½ teaspoon crushed cardamom pods
1¼ cups brown lentils
2 tomatoes, peeled and chopped
7 oz. spinach, cut into ribbons
juice of 1 lemon
sea salt and freshly ground black pepper

Serves 4

Heat the oil in a medium saucepan, add the onion, and cook for 5 minutes. Add the garlic, cumin or garam masala, curry powder, and cardamom, mix well, then cook for 3 minutes.

Add the brown lentils and 2 cups water, bring to a boil, reduce the heat, and simmer for about 20 minutes, stirring frequently.

When the lentils are soft, add the tomatoes, spinach, lemon juice, salt, and pepper. Stir well and serve hot or warm.

Blue cheese and rosemary polenta mash

Polenta is made from corn, so this comforting Italian dish is a great way to add variety to your carbohydrate intake. Serve it with a tomato and olive salad or, for big appetites, a broiled chop of lamb or pork.

1 cup quick-cooking polenta grains
4 tablespoons butter
2 tablespoons olive oil
1 cup Gorgonzola cheese, crumbled
1 cup mascarpone cheese
leaves from 1 sprig of rosemary, chopped
sea salt and freshly ground black pepper

Serves 4

Put 2¾ cups water in a saucepan and heat until simmering. Pour in the polenta and stir vigorously (to prevent it sticking to the bottom of the pan) with a wooden spoon for 5 minutes over a medium heat (the polenta will thicken and stiffen, making the stirring harder, but keep going otherwise you will have lumps).

Add the butter, olive oil, and Gorgonzola and mix well, then stir in the mascarpone, rosemary, and pepper. Taste and adjust the seasoning as necessary, bearing in mind that Gorgonzola is very salty. Mix well and serve.

Rich Tuscan bean soup

¼ cup olive oil
6 oz. pancetta or smoked bacon, diced
1 large onion, chopped
1 garlic clove, crushed and chopped
2 celery stalks, chopped
1 carrot, diced
3 cups canned chopped tomatoes
2 cups canned lima beans
½ vegetable or chicken bouillon cube
freshly ground black pepper

To serve

a bunch of flat-leaf parsley, chopped
¼ cup olive oil

Serves 4

Heat the oil in a skillet over medium heat. Add the pancetta and onion and cook for 5 minutes. Add the garlic, celery, and carrot and cook for another 5 minutes, mixing well.

Add the tomatoes, lima beans, a little pepper, and 1 cup water, then crumble in the bouillon cube. Bring the mixture to a boil, then lower the heat and simmer for 15 minutes.

Serve in heated soup bowls topped with the chopped parsley and a spoonful of olive oil. Serve with crusty country-style bread.

Mushroom risotto

They say that a risotto should be constantly stirred, but I don't totally agree that this is necessary. Time is too short. I do stir it frequently, but like to get on with something else in the kitchen at the same time.

4 cups chicken or vegetable stock
2 oz. dried mushrooms such as chanterelle, morel, shiitake, or porcini
1 tablespoon olive oil
4 tablespoons butter
1 garlic clove, crushed and chopped
1 onion, finely chopped
1½ cups risotto rice
⅓ cup dry white wine or vermouth
1 cup grated Parmesan cheese, plus 3 oz. extra, shaved or grated, to serve
sea salt and freshly ground black pepper

Serves 4

Put the stock and dried mushrooms in a saucepan and let soak for 10 minutes. Then slowly heat the stock to simmering point. Strain the mushrooms and return the stock to the saucepan to keep hot.

Melt the oil and half the butter in a large saucepan. Add the garlic and onion and cook over a medium heat until softened but not browned. Add the rice and stir until all the grains are coated with butter and oil.

Add a ladle of hot stock to the rice and mix well. When the rice has absorbed the liquid, add another ladle of stock and stir well. Repeat with the remaining stock, cooking the risotto for 15–20 minutes until all the liquid has been absorbed. Meanwhile, chop the mushrooms into smaller pieces as necessary.

Add the soaked mushrooms, white wine or vermouth, the remaining butter, and the grated Parmesan to the risotto. Season to taste with salt and pepper and mix gently over the heat for 2 minutes. Serve with a separate dish of the shaved or grated cheese to sprinkle over the top.

Salade Niçoise

One taste of this one and you will quickly forget all the other Salade Niçoises that you have ever eaten.

14 oz. fresh tuna steak, quartered
4 medium new potatoes, cooked and sliced
4 tomatoes, peeled and cut into wedges
4 oz. cooked green beans, trimmed and halved
1 red onion, sliced
4 baby romaine lettuce, quartered lengthwise
4 hard-cooked eggs, peeled and halved
4 anchovies, cut into long strips
12 black olives, pitted
a bunch of flat-leaf parsley, coarsely chopped
¼ cup olive oil
¼ cup balsamic vinegar
sea salt and freshly ground black pepper
1 lemon, cut into wedges, to serve

Serves 4

Heat a stove-top grill pan or broiler and cook the tuna for 1–2 minutes on each side. Remove from the heat and set aside in a warm place.

Put the cooked sliced potatoes in a bowl, then add the tomato wedges, beans, onion, lettuce, and eggs. Add the anchovies, olives, parsley, olive oil, balsamic vinegar, salt, and pepper. Mix carefully.

Serve the salad topped with the tuna and accompanied by wedges of lemon. Alternatively, the traditional way to serve this salad is to arrange groups of the ingredients on a large platter, then drizzle with the olive oil and vinegar.

top tip: To peel tomatoes, bring a saucepan of water to a boil, cut a cross in the skin at the base of each tomato, then plunge them into the boiling water for just 20 seconds. Drain, then peel the skin away when the tomatoes are cool enough to handle.

Risotto primavera

Risottos are very personal. Some like them very wet with the rice thoroughly cooked, others prefer a drier texture, or the rice still quite crunchy on the inside. My preference is for the rice to be slightly nutty and just wet enough to bind all the ingredients.

4 cups chicken or vegetable stock
½ cup (1 stick) butter
3 tablespoons olive oil
1 onion, diced
1 garlic clove, chopped
1¼ cups arborio or carnaroli rice
1¼ lb. mixed green vegetables, such as asparagus, fava beans, green beans, runner beans, green cabbage, peas, or spinach, all chopped into even-sized pieces.
⅓ cup dry vermouth or white wine
a bunch of flat-leaf parsley, chopped
1¼ cups freshly grated Parmesan cheese
sea salt and freshly ground black pepper

Serves 4

Pour the stock into a small saucepan and heat to simmering point.

In a large saucepan, melt the butter with the olive oil. Add the onion and garlic and cook over a low heat for 5 minutes until softened and translucent.

Add the rice, stirring with a wooden spoon to coat the grains thoroughly with butter and oil (this helps to make the risotto creamy).

Add a ladle of stock to the rice, mix well, and let simmer. When the liquid has almost evaporated, add another ladle of stock to the saucepan and stir thoroughly until it bubbles away. Continue, stirring the risotto as often as possible and adding more stock as needed.

After the risotto has been cooking for 12 minutes, add all the vegetables and mix well. Add the remaining stock, vermouth or white wine, salt, and pepper. Cook, stirring, for a further 4–5 minutes, then, just before serving, mix in the chopped parsley and grated Parmesan cheese.

dinner on a tray

Sitting in a comfortable chair and eating from a tray is one of the unsung pleasures of home life—indulgent, yet thoroughly casual. Big bowls of hearty food are best, served with a cool drink and an episode of televisual drama courtesy of your favorite soap opera.

comfort food

These recipes are for those days when you need an inside tummy hug. Choose from a cuddly classic pie, its rich steaming filling topped with homemade crumbly pastry, or a salad of silky avocado, tender chickpeas, and spinach bound together with creamy dressing, or that most wicked of desserts, banoffi—even the name is comforting to say.

Steak and mushroom pie

Nothing beats a good homemade pie with tender pieces of meat in a delicious gravy. This one is topped with crisp suet pastry.

Filling

3 tablespoons olive oil
2 onions, chopped
3 lb. stewing beef, cubed
1¾ cups button mushrooms
1 tablespoon flour
½ teaspoon dried mixed herbs
1 teaspoon Worcestershire sauce
1 teaspoon English mustard, or Dijon
1¾ cups beef stock
sea salt and freshly ground black pepper

Suet Pastry

1⅔ cups self-rising flour
4 oz. shredded suet or shortening

a 5-cup pie dish
Serves 4

To make the filling, heat the olive oil in a large skillet, add the onions, and sauté until softened but not browned. Transfer to a plate.

Add a little more oil to the skillet if needed, then add the meat and sauté until browned and sealed.

Add the mushrooms to the meat and sauté for about 5 minutes, then sprinkle in the flour and mix well to absorb all the oil.

Return the onions to the skillet and add the mixed herbs, Worcestershire sauce, mustard, salt, and pepper. Slowly pour in the stock, blending well. Bring to a boil, then lower the heat and simmer the mixture for 1½ hours.

When the meat is almost cooked, make the pastry. Sift the flour into a bowl, add the suet or shortening, salt, and pepper and mix well.

Add about 5 tablespoons water and mix with a round-bladed knife until the mixture forms a dough. A little more water may be needed, but take care not to add too much as it will make the pastry difficult to handle.

Transfer the cooked meat to the pie dish and set aside to cool.

Roll out the pastry to a circle larger than the pie dish. Wet the lip of the dish, then cut thin strips of pastry from the trimmings, and press onto the lip. Dampen the pastry lip. Lay the rolled pastry over the pie and flute the edge with your fingers to seal. Trim and make a small hole in the center.

Bake in a preheated oven at 425°F for about 35 minutes, until golden brown.

top tip: Suet pastry is best for savory pies as it is richer and more filling than a light flaky pastry. For vegetarian pies you can buy vegetarian suet.

Avocado and chickpea salad

This is a fresh, instant meal for lazy evenings. When buying avocados, make sure they are slightly soft to the touch and blemish-free.

2 eggs
8 oz. baby spinach, sliced into ribbons
2 cups canned chickpeas, rinsed and drained
2 ripe avocados, halved, pitted, sliced, and peeled
2 teaspoons sweet Spanish paprika
bread such as ciabatta or focaccia, to serve

Creamy chive dressing

juice of 1 lemon
3 tablespoons milk
2 tablespoons fromage frais or thick yogurt
a bunch of chives, chopped
sea salt and freshly ground black pepper
Serves 4

Simmer the eggs in a small saucepan of water for 8–9 minutes until hard-cooked. Drain, cool, peel, then cut into quarters and set aside.

To make the dressing, put the lemon juice in a bowl with the milk, fromage frais or yogurt, and chopped chives. Season generously with salt and pepper and stir until smooth.

Put the spinach, chickpeas, avocados, and eggs in a bowl. Sprinkle with the sweet paprika, then spoon over the dressing. Serve with fresh bread.

Tarte Tatin

This French upside-down tart of caramelized apples was invented by the Tatin sisters, who had a hotel in Lamotte-Beuvran. Maxim's in Paris took it into the culinary mainstream and stills serves it today, as do a great many restaurants around the world. Chefs like to experiment with alternative fruits such as bananas, clementines, and mango, but I think apple remains the best.

½ cup sugar
3 tablespoons butter
5 eating apples, peeled, cored, and quartered
cream or ice cream, to serve

Pastry

1 cup all-purpose flour
7 tablespoons butter
2 tablespoons sugar
2 egg yolks

an 8-inch ovenproof skillet or tarte Tatin pan

Serves 4

To make the pastry, put the flour in a mixing bowl, then rub in the butter with your fingertips until the mixture looks like breadcrumbs. Stir in the sugar.

Place the egg yolks in a small bowl and beat lightly with a fork. Add the yolks to the flour mixture and mix using a round-bladed knife until the dough binds together and forms a ball.

Dust your hands with flour. Working quickly, knead the dough until smooth on a lightly floured work surface, then wrap the dough in plastic and chill for 20 minutes.

To make the tarte, heat the skillet over medium heat, add the sugar and butter and melt until syrupy. Add the quartered apples and cook for a further 10–15 minutes. Remove from the heat when the apples are golden and the syrup is thick and smells of caramel.

Put the dough on a lightly floured surface and roll it out to a circle slightly larger than the skillet. Lay the dough on top of the apples and tuck the edges in around the sides of the skillet.

Transfer the skillet to a preheated oven at 400°F and cook for 40 minutes; check after 20 minutes and reduce the heat if the tart seems to be browning too quickly.

Remove the tart from the oven. Put a heatproof plate over the top of the skillet and quickly turn it upside down, taking care not to drip any of the hot juices on your skin. Lift the skillet off the pie—the pastry will be underneath and the caramelized apples will be on top.

Slice and serve warm with cream or ice cream.

Banoffi pie

Very rich and delicious, banoffi pie is only for those with an ardent sweet tooth. I boil up several cans of condensed milk at once, then keep them in the cupboard until needed.

¾ cup canned sweetened condensed milk
10 oz. graham crackers
½ cup butter
3 bananas
1 cup heavy cream
1½ oz. good-quality bitter chocolate
  (60 percent cocoa solids)

an 8-inch false-bottom tart pan
Serves 4

Put the unopened can of condensed milk in a large saucepan. Cover with water, bring to a boil, then reduce the heat and simmer for 3 hours. Check the water level from time to time and top up as necessary. Let cool overnight.

Put the graham crackers in a blender or food processor and blend until crushed.

Melt the butter in a small saucepan. Add the cracker crumbs and mix well. Pour the buttered crumbs into the tart pan and spread evenly over the bottom and up the sides to form a pie crust. Transfer to the refrigerator to set.

Open the cooled can of condensed milk to reveal the sticky caramel. Spoon it into the pie crust and spread out evenly.

Slice the bananas and arrange them on top of the caramel. Whip the cream in a large bowl until soft peaks form, then use it to cover the pie.

Grate the chocolate and sprinkle it over the cream. Refrigerate until ready to serve.

top tip: When flipping the cooked tarte Tatin out of the skillet onto a plate, be sure to protect your hands and arms with proper oven gloves. The faster you turn the pan over, the less likely it is that the hot cooking juices will escape and burn you, but keep a firm grip on the skillet and plate.

one-pot meals

Bouillabaisse

Buy only the freshest and best-quality fish for this classic Mediterranean dish. From the white fish family you can choose from bream, cod, halibut, monkfish, red mullet, snapper, sole, or whiting. If using an oily fish, salmon is the preferred variety. Good bouillabaisse also features other seafood such as shrimp, mussels, and clams. If you're feeling rich, you can also include a lobster.

Ask the store to clean, scale, and fillet the fish and keep all the bones to make the stock. Make sure they remove all the scales (this is especially important for snapper).

½ cup olive oil
1 large onion, diced
2 leeks, finely sliced
2 garlic cloves, crushed and chopped
1 small head of Florence fennel, diced
3 cups passata or crushed tomatoes
4 cups fish stock (see below)
a sprig of thyme
1 fresh bay leaf
a pinch of saffron threads
4 lb. fish and shellfish, cleaned, scaled, and filleted, heads and bones reserved
sea salt and freshly ground black pepper
warm crusty bread, to serve

Fish stock
fish bones and heads
1 onion, sliced
1 carrot, sliced
1 leek, sliced
5 sprigs of parsley
1 fresh bay leaf
Serves 4

To make the fish stock, put all the fish bones, heads, and the shells of any seafood in a large saucepan or Dutch oven. Cover with water, add the onion, carrot, leek, parsley sprigs, bay leaf, salt, and pepper. Bring the mixture to a boil and simmer for just 20 minutes, skimming off the foam from time to time.

Strain the stock reserving 3 cups to use in this recipe—you can cool and freeze the remainder for use in another dish.

To make the bouillabaisse, heat the olive oil in a large skillet. Add the onion, leeks, garlic, and fennel and sauté the vegetables for 5 minutes without letting them brown.

Add the passata or crushed tomatoes, thyme, bay leaf, saffron, fish stock, salt, and pepper. Bring to a boil and simmer for 10 minutes.

Add the cleaned pieces of fish and shellfish and cook for 4 minutes.

Carefully lift out the fish fillets and shellfish and divide between 4 large bowls. Ladle over the rich tomato liquid and serve with warm crusty bread.

Spaghetti carbonara
Easy but truly delicious, this Italian classic never seems to lose its popularity.

1 tablespoon olive oil
7 oz. smoked bacon, cut into strips
1 garlic clove, crushed and chopped
10 oz. dried spaghetti
⅓ cup heavy cream
4 egg yolks
1 cup freshly grated Parmesan cheese
sea salt and freshly ground black pepper
Serves 4

Heat the oil in a large saucepan, add the bacon, and cook over a medium heat for 3 minutes. Add the garlic and cook for a further minute. Remove from the pan and set aside.

Fill the pan with boiling water. Add the dried spaghetti, stirring well to stop it sticking. Return to a boil, then simmer for 9 minutes.

When cooked, drain the spaghetti and return it to the pan. Add the cooked bacon mixture, cream, egg yolks, Parmesan, salt, and pepper. Mix well over the heat for 1–2 minutes to coat the pasta in the sauce and cook the eggs.

Serve immediately in warm bowls.

top tip: If you prefer not to eat meat, you can replace the bacon in this sauce with a variety of mushrooms, such as cremini and button or treat yourself to wild mushrooms.

Steaming bowls of delicious goodness, one-pot meals can be some of the most comforting and easy, with the added bonus that there is only one pan to wash afterwards. These wonderful dishes for adults and children take their inspiration from all round the world, from the Mediterranean to Southeast Asia, proving that simple home cooking need never be dull.

Butternut and cashew soup

The color and velvety-smooth flavor of this soup make it a winner with the whole family. For special occasions, serve with Parmesan wafers (page 137).

¼ cup olive oil
4 tablespoons butter
1 onion, chopped
1 butternut squash, about 2 lb., peeled, seeded, and coarsely chopped
1 teaspoon medium curry powder
⅔ cup milk
1 cup cashews, coarsely chopped
sea salt and freshly ground black pepper

Serves 4

Heat the olive oil and butter in a large saucepan over a medium heat. Add the onion and cook for 5 minutes until soft but not browned.

Add the chopped butternut, curry powder, and a little salt and pepper, then cook for 5 minutes.

Pour in 2 cups water and the milk, then bring the mixture to a boil, lower the heat, and simmer for 30 minutes.

Add the cashews and cool briefly. Working in batches if necessary, transfer the soup to a blender or food processor and purée until smooth and thick. Alternatively, use a stick blender and purée the soup in the saucepan.

Reheat the soup as necessary. Taste and adjust the seasoning to your liking, then serve hot.

Green bean and herb broth

I prefer this soup served on its own—it makes a perfect light meal. If you need a dish that is a little more filling, add some pasta or noodles at the same time as the stock. The vegetables and herbs in this soup need only quick, light cooking to bring out their delicate flavors.

¼ cup olive oil
1 onion, very finely sliced
4 cups vegetable stock
1 garlic clove, crushed
8 oz. green beans, cut into 1-inch pieces
8 oz. runner beans, cut into 1-inch pieces
8 oz. shelled fava beans, peeled, or peas

sea salt and freshly ground black pepper
a bunch of chervil, coarsely chopped
a bunch of dill, coarsely chopped
Serves 4

Heat the olive oil in a large saucepan or Dutch oven. Add the sliced onion and cook over a low heat for 10 minutes without browning. Add the garlic and cook gently for a further 5 minutes.

Pour in the stock and add salt and pepper. Bring to a boil, reduce the heat, and simmer for 5 minutes.

Add all the beans to the soup and simmer for 4 minutes, then add the chopped fresh herbs and cook for a further 2 minutes only. Serve immediately.

When I want something light but flavorsome, filling but not too heavy, a generous bowl of quickly made noodle stir-fry, or a pure and delicate vegetable broth is the perfect choice. Healthy, fast, and delicious—what more could you want for supper?

Vegetable noodle stir-fry

When making this dish, prepare all the vegetables in advance, so the stir-fry can be quickly and easily put together. Don't overcook the vegetables—they are better when crunchy and brightly colored. You can change the vegetables according to what's in your fridge or what your children like, but always use the onion, garlic, ginger, and chile.

¼ cup sunflower or peanut oil
1 garlic clove, crushed
2 inches fresh ginger, diced
1 onion, finely sliced
1 chile, finely chopped
4 oz. thin noodles, such as egg noodles
2 pak choi, about 8 oz., coarsely chopped
1 leek, cut into strips
1½ cups bean sprouts, rinsed and trimmed
1½ cups sliced mushrooms
3 tablespoons soy sauce
juice of 1 lime
a bunch of cilantro, chopped
Serves 4

Heat the oil in a wok. Add the garlic, ginger, onion, and chile and cook over a medium heat, stirring constantly.

Bring a large saucepan of water to a boil. Add the noodles and cook for 1 minute if fresh or 3 minutes if dried. Drain thoroughly.

Add the pak choi, leek, bean sprouts, and mushrooms to the wok and stir-fry for 2-3 minutes.

Add the soy sauce, lime juice, and noodles and use 2 spoons to mix the vegetables and noodles together. Top with the chopped cilantro and serve immediately in bowls with chopsticks instead of cutlery.

Thai meatballs and noodles

Here is a lovely and warming noodle broth with delicious chicken meatballs. The blend of flavors is quite heavenly in this one-pot dish and I'm sure you will want to make it often. If you don't like very hot chiles, use a milder variety, such as jalapeño, instead of the fiery bird's eye chile.

1 lb. chicken, finely ground
1 small onion, diced
2 inches fresh ginger, peeled and chopped
2 bird's eye chiles, seeded and diced
2 garlic cloves, chopped
2¾ cups chicken stock
10 oz. noodles, such as egg noodles
sea salt
a bunch of cilantro chopped, to serve
Serves 4

Put the chicken, onion, ginger, chiles, garlic, and salt in a bowl and mix with your hands (this is much easier than using a spoon). Divide the mixture into 16 equal-sized portions and roll into balls using wet hands.

Put the chicken stock in a large saucepan and bring to a boil. Carefully add the chicken meatballs and simmer for about 10 minutes.

Add the noodles and push down to submerge them in the chicken stock. Cook for 4-8 minutes, or according to the package instructions.

Spoon the noodles, meatballs, and broth into large bowls and serve topped with the chopped cilantro.

top tip: Finely grinding the chicken helps bind the meatballs together. Other meats such as pork or beef, or some ground white fish or shrimp could also be used to make these dumplings.

Heat the olive oil in a paella pan or large skillet. Add the onion, garlic, and chorizo. Cook over a low heat until the onion is softened and translucent, about 5 minutes.

Add the chicken pieces and cook for about 5 minutes on each side until lightly browned.

Add the rice, saffron, and stock to the skillet and mix well. Bring the mixture to a boil, reduce the heat, and simmer for 15 minutes, stirring so the rice doesn't stick to the base of the skillet. Add some more stock if needed.

Add the white wine, mussels, shrimp, squid, salt, and pepper. Cover with a lid or piece of foil and cook, without stirring, for a further 8–10 minutes.

Squeeze the juice from 1 lemon and cut the other into wedges. Stir the juice into the paella. Top with the chopped parsley and serve from the pan with lemon wedges on the side.

Steamed syrup pudding

An easy-to-make winter classic, this pudding is always a winner. You could omit the syrup and use the same volume of honey, jam, lemon curd, or chopped preserved ginger if preferred.

1 cup (2 sticks) butter, softened
1¼ cups sugar
3 eggs
2½ cups self-rising flour
2 tablespoons milk
¼ cup corn syrup
vanilla ice cream, to serve

a 4-cup porcelain pudding basin, buttered
Serves 4

Put the butter and sugar in a medium mixing bowl and beat with a wooden spoon until pale and creamy. Add the eggs one at a time and beat until blended.

Sift the flour over the egg mixture and fold in. Add the milk and continue folding the mixture until smooth.

Pour the corn syrup into the buttered pudding basin. Spoon the sponge mixture on top. Cover with waxed paper and secure with kitchen twine.

Sit the pudding basin in a large saucepan. Pour in boiling water until it comes about halfway up the sides of the basin. Cover and simmer gently for 1 hour, topping up with more boiling water as necessary.

Carefully remove the pudding basin from the saucepan and peel off the paper. Put a large serving plate on top of the basin and turn the pudding over, giving it a gentle shake to release from the mold.

Cut the pudding at the table and serve on small plates or in dessert bowls, accompanied by the ice cream.

Paella

This wonderful Spanish dish is very easy to make and a joy to eat. Don't be put off by the long list of ingredients—they are all readily available from your local supermarket. On special occasions, serve the paella with a mixed leaf salad, followed by fresh fruit and Spanish cheeses for a very stylish meal (and a happy cook).

2 tablespoons olive oil
1 onion, diced
2 garlic cloves, crushed and chopped
4 oz. chorizo sausage, thickly sliced
4 skinless chicken pieces, trimmed
1 cup long-grain rice
a large pinch of saffron threads
2¾ cups chicken stock
1 cup white wine
12 mussels, cleaned
8 large shrimp
4 oz. squid, cleaned and cut into rings
sea salt and freshly ground black pepper
2 lemons
a bunch of flat-leaf parsley, chopped
Serves 4

elegant drinks and finger food

The idea of attempting a glamorous and sophisticated cocktail party at home sends most of us into a panic and often results in a quick phone call to the caterers. Trust me: you can invite a few people and serve any of the following recipes for a sensational party that your friends will remember for a long time—for the style and elegance of its drinks, food, and company.

Brazen Martini

¹/₄ cup Bison vodka
2 tablespoons Parfait d' Amour violet liqueur
ice cubes, for shaking

a cocktail shaker
Makes 1

Fill the shaker with ice cubes. Add the vodka and violet liqueur and shake until well blended and chilled. Strain the mixture into a cocktail glass and serve.

Blueberry Martini

8-10 blueberries
¹/₄ cup vodka
2 tablespoons crème de cassis
ice cubes, for shaking

a cocktail shaker
Makes 1

Put the blueberries in the shaker and crush them with a pestle or the back of a spoon.

Fill the shaker with ice and add the vodka and crème de cassis. Shake until well blended and chilled. Use a fine sieve to strain the mixture into a cocktail glass. Serve.

Parmesan wafers

These wafers taste fantastic and are so easy to make—yes, there really is only one ingredient!

2³/₄ cups Parmesan cheese, grated

a baking tray, lined with waxed paper
Makes 20

Pile teaspoons of the grated Parmesan on the paper-lined baking tray and flatten gently to give equal-sized rounds.

Bake in a preheated oven at 375°F for 5 minutes—the cheese will melt, bubble, and turn golden.

Remove the paper from the baking tray with the wafers still on it. Replace with another sheet of paper and repeat with the remaining cheese.

When the wafers are cool, remove and store in an airtight container until needed.

top tip: To ring the changes, add a little coarsely ground black pepper, chopped rosemary, or some finely chopped pine nuts to the cheese.

Avruga baby baked potatoes

Avruga, like little black pearls, is herring roe and has a lovely mellow, slightly smoky flavor. If it is not available, use other fish eggs such as salmon (keta) or trout, or splash out on fine caviar.

10 baby potatoes
¹/₂ head of celery
¹/₂ cup sour cream
4 oz. avruga, keta, trout roe, or caviar

a baking tray, oiled
Makes 10 of each

Put the potatoes on the baking tray and cook in a preheated oven at 350°F for 15 minutes. Remove and let cool for 10 minutes.

Cut small, deep crosses in the potatoes, then squeeze to open out slightly. Spoon a small amount of sour cream in each potato and top with a spoonful of avruga.

Cut the celery into 3-inch lengths and put a spoonful of avruga at the end of each one. Serve.

top tip: If you're catering for a lot of people, serve the soured cream and avruga in small bowls with spoons. Cut the cooked baby potatoes and squeeze open, but let guests fill their own.

Sea Breeze

¼ cup vodka
½ cup cranberry juice
¼ cup grapefruit juice
ice cubes, to serve
Makes 1

Fill a highball glass with ice, add the vodka, and then the fruit juices. Stir and serve.

Cosmopolitan

2 tablespoons Absolut-citron vodka
2 tablespoons Cointreau
¼ cup cranberry juice
2 tablespoons freshly squeezed lime juice
ice cubes, for shaking

a cocktail shaker
Makes 1

Fill the shaker with ice cubes. Add the alcohol and juices and shake until well blended and chilled. Strain into a cocktail glass and serve.

French 75

2 tablespoons gin
2 tablespoons freshly squeezed lemon juice
a dash of sugar syrup
⅓ cup chilled champagne, plus extra to serve
ice cubes, for shaking

a cocktail shaker
Makes 1

Put the gin, lemon juice, and sugar syrup in the cocktail shaker. Add the ice and shake.

Pour into a champagne flute, add the champagne, and top up with more champagne before serving.

Pimm's Cocktail

Use your own selection of fresh fruit, but orange, cucumber, and mint are traditional.

¼ cup Pimm's No. 1
1 cup lemonade
1 slice lemon
2 sprigs of mint
2 slices cucumber, cut lengthwise
ice cubes, to serve
Makes 1

Fill a highball glass with ice and add each of the ingredients in turn. Serve cold.

Crispy Noodles

These are also called *mee krob*—they are always popular, so be sure to make plenty.

sunflower oil, for deep-frying, plus
    1 tablespoon extra for stir-frying
2 oz. rice vermicelli
1 onion, finely diced
1 garlic clove, crushed and chopped
1 inch fresh ginger, peeled and diced
1 fresh red chile, diced
a bunch of cilantro, chopped
a bunch of chives, chopped
2 mini lettuces, such as mini romaine
Makes 20

Fill a wok one-third full of oil and heat. To test if the oil is hot enough to begin cooking, add a piece of vermicelli: it should puff up immediately, if it sinks to the bottom, heat the oil a little more.

Add the vermicelli in small handfuls, turning it with tongs to help it puff up evenly, then remove to a plate lined with crumpled paper towels. Pour the oil into a heatproof container.

Wipe out the wok and return to the heat. Add 1 tablespoon oil, then the onion, garlic, ginger, and chile. Stir-fry for 5 minutes.

Turn off the heat, add the cooked noodles to the wok and mix well. Stir in the herbs.

Break the lettuce leaves away from the stem. Fill them with spoonfuls of the noodle mixture, arrange on a plate to serve.

Goat cheese and pepper crostini

Buy a smooth and creamy goat cheese that has no rind. They are usually sold in a pot.

1 thin French breadstick (ficelle)
6 oz. fresh creamy goat cheese
4 roasted red bell peppers, peeled
20 spears Thai asparagus, cooked and refreshed
sea salt and freshly ground black pepper
olive oil, for brushing

a baking tray
Serves 20

To make the crostini, slice the bread diagonally into 20 thin slices. Brush with olive oil, then add salt and pepper. Cook in a preheated oven at 375°F for 5 minutes until golden.

Arrange the crostini on a plate and spread with goat cheese. Cut the roasted peppers into thin strips. Arrange a strip of pepper and a spear of asparagus on each crostini and serve.

Mojito

1 lime, cut into 16 pieces
enough mint tips to half-fill the glass
2 teaspoons sugar
¼ cup dark rum
crushed ice, to serve
soda water, to taste (optional)
Makes 1

Put the lime and mint into an old-fashioned glass, then sprinkle with sugar. Using a pestle or the back of a spoon, crush the lime, mint, and sugar together until the sugar has completely dissolved.

Fill the glass with crushed ice, add the rum, and stir briefly. Add soda water to taste if desired.

Chinese duck forks

These irresistible duck morsels are sweet, delicious, and look wonderful. Serve them skewered on little forks, or on some Chinese porcelain spoons (which don't cost much, but look terrific).

1 duck breast, skinned
3 scallions, cut into 2-inch pieces, then finely sliced lengthwise
4 inches cucumber, peeled, seeded, cut into 2-inch pieces, then finely sliced lengthwise

Chinese marinade
2 tablespoons soy sauce
2 tablespoons dry sherry

1 tablespoon sugar
2 whole star anise
⅛ inch fresh ginger, chopped
¼ cup plum sauce

12 forks or Chinese porcelain spoons
Serves 12

Put all the marinade ingredients in a small nonstick pan or skillet, and heat until simmering.

Add the duck breast and simmer very gently for 6 minutes on each side. Remove from the heat, cover, and cool. When cool, slice the duck very thinly crosswise. Reserve the marinade.

Lay out the sliced duck breast, place a few scallions and cucumber strips at one end, and roll up tightly into parcels. Push onto the forks or lay in the Chinese spoons, drizzle with a little of the reserved marinade, and serve.

Mexican shrimp wraps

These canapés are visually stunning. The shrimp can be replaced with chicken, rare beef, or grated fresh vegetables such as carrots and radishes. A long, cool Mojito is the perfect accompaniment to these wraps.

2 flour tortillas, 8 inches diameter

Salsa
1 jalapeño chile, seeded and finely diced
½ red onion, finely diced
1 garlic clove, finely diced
2 tomatoes, peeled, seeded, and diced
3 tablespoons sour cream
sea salt and freshly ground black pepper

Filling
½ avocado, peeled and sliced
juice of ½ lime
3 oz. cooked and peeled shrimp
a small bunch of arugula
makes 20

To make the salsa, put all the ingredients in a bowl and stir well.

Heat the tortillas in a dry skillet, then put on a large chopping board. Divide the salsa between them and spread out evenly. Top with avocado and sprinkle with a little lime juice. Scatter the shrimp and arugula over the tortillas.

Roll up tightly and wrap in plastic, twisting the ends to secure. Chill for 30 minutes, then slice each roll into 10 pieces and arrange on a platter.

Lobby Dazzler

3–4 kumquats, quartered
2 teaspoons sugar
¼ cup Absolut-kurant vodka or vodka
crushed ice, to serve
Makes 1

Put the kumquats in an old-fashioned glass and sprinkle with sugar. Using a pestle or the back of a spoon, crush the kumquat and sugar together until the sugar completely dissolves and all the fruit juice is released.

Fill the glass with crushed ice, add the vodka, and stir briefly before serving.

party time

Invite lots of friends, fill a table with food and drink and let people help themselves. Sounds easy, and yes it can be—but to me the food is all-important. I have put together a great-tasting feast for you here, so pile the plates high, put all the silver, napkins, and glasses on the table, and let the party begin.

It takes organization followed by more organization to throw a memorable party, but it can be achieved with ease if you follow these helpful tips. Start with a date, venue, list of friends, and style of party, then send the invitations.

Keep the food simple and limit the courses. Choose dishes that can be made in advance and presented as a buffet so that you need not spend the evening locked in the kitchen. I always supplement the cooking with a good salad, ripe soft cheese, breads, and a large platter of prepared fresh fruit placed on the table at the end of the meal for guests to help themselves.

Enjoy decorating your space with items related to the theme of the party. Empty a room, fill it with rugs, a large low table, soft pillows, scented candles, maybe some rose petals scattered over the table. Finally, open your doors and party!

top tip: Shop wisely at a good gourmet store to enhance your menu. Buy antipasto and vegetables to add to the salad; select a fine cheese board, and don't skimp on the fresh bread.

menu

Artichoke and cheese tart

Peppered beef with watercress salad

Tiramisu

Cabernet Sauvignon

Artichoke and cheese tart

This flexible and remarkably easy tart can be topped with all sorts of vegetables and any of your favorite cheeses—the combinations are limitless, so don't hesitate to experiment.

2 packages frozen puff pastry (1 lb.), thawed
5 roasted bell peppers, cut into 1-inch strips
3 jars artichoke hearts in oil, 10 oz. each
6 onions, sliced
1 lb. baby leeks, trimmed and washed
1 lb. cheese, coarsely grated or crumbled
1 egg yolk, beaten
3–4 tablespoons extra virgin olive oil
sea salt and freshly ground black pepper

2 baking trays, lightly oiled
Serves 20

Roll out each package of pastry and put one piece on each baking tray. Prick all over with a fork, then bake in a preheated oven at 350°F for 20 minutes.

Put the roasted bell peppers in a large bowl with the artichokes, onions, leeks, cheese, salt, and pepper. Mix well.

Remove the cooked pastry from the oven, then brush all over with the beaten egg yolk.

Divide the filling between the pastry sheets and spread out evenly. Return the tarts to the oven and bake for a further 30 minutes.

Serve hot or at room temperature, lightly drizzled with a little extra virgin olive oil.

top tip: This tart can be partially baked one day ahead. Cook the pastry, cover with plastic wrap, and store in an airtight container until needed. Mix all the topping ingredients, cover, and chill. Then assemble on the day— if you make it completely the day before, you run the risk of the pastry becoming soggy.

Peppered beef with watercress salad

Fillet is the finest cut of beef but if you need something a little more economical, try roasting a piece of sirloin.

6 egg whites
3 lb. beef fillet or sirloin, well trimmed
⅓ cup coarsely crushed peppercorns
¼ cup mixed mustard seeds
2 lb. vine tomatoes
6 bunches of watercress, about 4 oz. each
1 lb. mixed lettuce leaves, torn into pieces
30 hard-cooked quail eggs or small hen eggs, halved

Orange dressing
1 tablespoon sugar
juice and zest of 3 oranges
2 tablespoons balsamic vinegar
3 tablespoons liquid honey
2 garlic cloves, crushed and chopped

¾ cup sunflower oil
sea salt and freshly ground black pepper

a roasting pan
a baking tray, greased
Serves 20

Lightly beat the egg whites in a large bowl for 2 minutes. Add the beef and turn until it is well coated with the egg whites.

Mix the peppercorns and mustard on a flat plate, then roll the beef in the mixture to make a crust.

Put the tomatoes on the baking tray and cook in a preheated oven at 375°F for 1 hour. Meanwhile, pour the olive oil into the roasting pan and heat in the oven.

When the oil is hot, add the beef, turning to coat in the hot oil. Roast at the top of the oven for 45 minutes for rare meat, 1 hour for medium, and 1½ hours for well done. Remove the tomatoes from the oven when cooked and set aside to cool. Set the meat aside to rest for about 10 minutes.

When ready to serve, mix the watercress with the other leaves and put on a serving platter with the tomatoes and quail eggs.

To make the dressing, put the sugar in a bowl with the orange zest and juice, vinegar, honey, garlic, salt, and pepper. Beat in the oil with a fork or stick blender.

Slice the beef and arrange on the salad. Just before serving, drizzle with the dressing.

Robust food with chunky textures and distinct flavors is best for lively parties and suits whatever kind of alcohol your friends are drinking. Make sure you offer plenty of water and other non-alcoholic drinks too so that all guests feel welcome.

Tiramisu

Foolproof and very quick to prepare, tiramisu is a wonderful dessert to serve a large group of people—it can be made in advance, doesn't need cooking or heating, and tastes so delicious that it is universally welcomed. I like to make it with amaretti and present it in 20 groovy glasses instead of one very large serving bowl.

50 amaretti cookies, crushed
¾ cup Kahlúa or other coffee liqueur
⅓ cup brandy
½ cup strong black coffee
2 lb. mascarpone cheese
12 eggs separated
½ cup sugar
8 oz. bitter chocolate, grated, or ¼ cup unsweetened cocoa powder

20 glasses or a 12-inch square serving dish.
Serves 20

Arrange a quarter of the crushed amaretti cookies at the bottom of the glasses or serving dish. Mix the Kahlúa in a small bowl with the brandy and coffee, and pour a quarter of this mixture over the crushed amarettis.

Put the mascarpone, egg yolks, and sugar in a bowl and beat until smooth. In a separate bowl, beat the egg whites until stiff, then fold into the mascarpone mixture.

Spoon a quarter of the mixture over the amarettis, then repeat the layers 3 times, finishing with a layer of mascarpone mixture.

Sprinkle the chocolate or cocoa over the top of the tiramisu and refrigerate overnight. Serve chilled or at room temperature.

top tip: Instead of topping the tiramisu with grated chocolate, melt the chocolate in a plastic bag tied securely to close. Make a small hole in one corner and pipe 20 squiggles onto waxed paper. Let set, then stick the chocolate shapes upright into the individual tiramisus.

dinner for friends

Mulled wine

Warm your house and make your friends' hearts glow with this beautiful spicy drink also known as *glühwein*. If making it for a big party, add more wine and sugar to the pan as the evening wears on.

2 bottles red wine, 3 cups each
8 whole cloves
2 oranges
3 tablespoons brown sugar
2 inches fresh ginger, peeled and chopped
1 cinnamon stick
½ teaspoon freshly grated nutmeg
Serves 4

Pour the red wine into a medium saucepan. Stick the cloves into the oranges, then cut each orange into quarters. Add to the pan, together with the sugar, ginger, cinnamon, and nutmeg.

Heat the mixture to simmering point and simmer for 8–10 minutes, then serve hot.

Green chicken curry

A great meal to serve for all occasions, this dish will improve with time so make it the night before, reheat well, and add the herbs just before serving. The coconut milk gives a beautiful silky quality to the fragrant sauce.

¼ cup sunflower or peanut oil
1 onion, sliced
2 inches fresh ginger, peeled and sliced
2 garlic cloves, crushed and chopped
2 stalks lemongrass, finely sliced
2 green chiles, chopped
8 skinless chicken pieces
2 teaspoon medium-hot curry powder
4 kaffir lime leaves or a strip of lime peel
¾ cup coconut milk
sea salt and freshly ground black pepper

To serve
a bunch of basil leaves, torn
a bunch of cilantro, chopped
steamed Thai rice
Serves 4

Heat the oil in a large saucepan. Add the onion, ginger, garlic, lemongrass, and chiles and sauté over a low heat for 10 minutes.

Add the chicken and cook for 5 minutes to seal on all sides. Mix in the curry powder, kaffir lime leaves or lime peel, salt, and pepper.

Stir in the coconut milk and ¾ cup boiling water, then cover and simmer for 40 minutes. Do not boil or the coconut milk will curdle.

Spoon the curry into a serving dish, top with the basil and cilantro and serve with Thai rice.

You've known each other for years and see them often, but still there's few people you'd rather cook for. Supper could be two fun courses served at the kitchen counter, or something more traditional eaten at the family table. You want to treat them but, whatever the menu, they'll love it because they are really there to see you.

Salmon fishcakes

If salmon is unavailable use cod, smoked fish, or a mixture of crab and shrimp to make these fishcakes. It is worth doubling the quantity and freezing the extras.

13 oz. skinless salmon fillets
14 oz. cooked mashed potatoes
3 scallions, finely sliced
a bunch of parsley, chopped

3 eggs
$^2/_3$ cup all-purpose flour, plus extra for dusting
1$^1/_4$ cups breadcrumbs
1$^1/_4$ cups sunflower oil, for frying
sea salt and freshly ground black pepper

To serve
1 lemon, cut into quarters
hollandaise sauce (see opposite)

Serves 4

Put the salmon in a medium-sized ovenproof dish. Cover with a lid and cook in a preheated oven at 350°F for 10 minutes.

Remove the fish from the oven and let cool, still covered. When cool, flake the flesh with a fork.

Put the mashed potatoes in a mixing bowl. Add the flaked salmon, scallions, parsley, salt, and pepper. Stir well.

Put 1 of the eggs in a small bowl and beat with a fork. Stir it into the fish mixture.

Beat the remaining 2 eggs in the same small bowl and set aside. Put the flour in a separate clean bowl and put the breadcrumbs on a plate.

Divide the fish mixture into 8 equal portions and, using floured hands, shape them into patties.

Dust each patty lightly with flour, then dip it into the beaten eggs, and finally cover with the breadcrumbs, pressing them into the surface. Place on a large plate until needed.

Repeat until all the fish patties are coated with egg and breadcrumbs.

Heat the sunflower oil in a skillet, add the fishcakes, and cook over a medium heat until golden on both sides, approximately 5 minutes.

Serve the cooked fishcakes with lemon wedges and a pitcher of warm hollandaise sauce.

Hollandaise sauce

This recipe may be wicked, but to me it's the king of sauces. I think everyone should eat it once in a while and just forget about the calories. As a variation, add some finely chopped fresh herbs such as basil, chives, parsley, sage, thyme, or watercress at the final moment. Note that the proper pepper to use in this sauce is freshly ground white pepper, not black.

1 cup (2 sticks) butter
2 egg yolks
2 tablespoons white wine vinegar
juice of ½ lemon
sea salt and freshly ground white pepper
Serves 4

Put the butter in a small saucepan and melt it slowly over a low heat.

Put the eggs in a heatproof pitcher and beat using a stick blender. With the blender still running, pour in the melted butter in a steady stream.

Bring a large saucepan of water to the boil, then reduce the heat to low and set the pitcher over the water. Heat the egg mixture for 10 minutes.

Blend the mixture again (it should have thickened with the warmth), then blend in the vinegar, lemon juice, salt, and pepper.

Cover with plastic wrap, letting it sit on the surface of the sauce to prevent a skin forming. Leave over the pan of warm water until needed.

Baked and glazed ham

Ham is an easy dish to prepare for a large gathering and children love it. Buy a ready-boned ham to make carving simple. A 2-lb. piece will leave you some extra to serve in salads and sandwiches the following week.

2 lb. cured ham, soaked
2 tablespoons English or Dijon mustard
2 tablespoons brown sugar
1 teaspoon crushed cloves
freshly ground black pepper

a roasting pan, lightly oiled
Serves 4

Put the ham in the roasting pan and cover with heavy-duty aluminun foil, pleating it down the middle to make a tent. Cook in a preheated oven at 325°F for 1 hour.

Remove from the oven and discard the foil. Drain off the cooking juices (keep them for soups) and peel off the skin, leaving a layer of fat. Using a knife, score the fat with a criss-cross pattern.

Spread the mustard evenly over the ham. Mix the sugar, cloves, and pepper in a small bowl, then sprinkle the mixture all over the ham, pressing it down into the fat with your hands.

Return the ham to the oven and bake for a further 20 minutes. Serve hot, warm, or cold.

Potatoes boulangère

Finely sliced potatoes cooked in a subtle stock and allowed to dry and crisp on top: edible heaven.

2 lb. mealy potatoes, sliced
2 onions, finely sliced
1¼ cups hot chicken, beef, or vegetable stock
2 tablespoons butter, finely diced
sea salt and freshly ground black pepper

a 9-inch shallow, ovenproof dish, buttered
Serves 4

Put a layer of potatoes in the buttered dish, then add a layer of onions. Season well, then repeat the layers until all the ingredients are used. Finish with a neat layer of potatoes overlapping each other and push down firmly.

Pour on the hot stock and dot with the butter. Bake in a preheated oven at 350°F for 1½ hours or until the top is golden brown and crunchy and the potatoes are soft right through when tested with the point of a knife.

Quick French apple tart

To make this tart sensational, do make sure the apples are sliced as finely as possible and they are arranged neatly, "like well-trained soldiers."

8 oz. ready-made puff pastry

1 egg, beaten

4 red eating apples

2 tablespoons butter, melted

2 tablespoons brown sugar

½ teaspoon ground cinnamon

a baking tray, lightly buttered

Serves 4

Roll out the pastry to a rectangle 12 x 7 inches. Put on the baking tray and brush all over with the egg.

Cut the apples into quarters, removing the cores. Slice thinly and arrange in rows on top of the pastry, leaving a 2-inch gap around the edges.

Drizzle the melted butter over the apples, sprinkle with sugar, and dust with cinnamon.

Brush the edges of the pastry with the remaining egg wash, then fold them inwards and gently press down.

Bake the tart in a preheated oven at 400°F for about 30 minutes. Reduce the temperature to 350°F and bake for another 15 minutes until the tart is well risen, crisp, and golden all over.

Serve hot or at room temperature with whipped heavy cream, clotted cream, scoops of good-quality vanilla ice cream, or homemade custard.

Watermelon granita

On a warm summer day, this granita is cooling and very refreshing to eat. The fresh ginger gives it a subtle but delicious twist.

2 lb. peeled and seeded watermelon flesh
3 inches fresh ginger, peeled and finely diced, to serve
Serves 4

Check that all the seeds are removed from the watermelon, then put the flesh in a blender and purée until smooth.

Transfer to an ice cream machine and churn according to the manufacturer's instructions until crystallized and firm. Alternatively, put the fruit purée in a plastic box in the freezer and, every 20 minutes, remove and break up the ice crystals with a fork. Repeat at least 3 times to achieve a good, firm consistency.

When frozen, serve the watermelon granita in chilled glasses, topped with the finely diced ginger.

twilight barbecue

Outdoor entertaining is not restricted to those with a large garden or to country-dwellers. Roof terraces have become very hip in the city and, in summer, they provide a great opportunity to have friends over to watch the sun set over dinner. This menu, with its distinctly Middle Eastern flavor, is specially designed for such an occasion.

Turkish toasted bread

Indian and Middle Eastern stores stock a wide variety of unusual and delicious items. My local store has a great selection of at least eight different breads, as well as the healthiest herbs you have ever seen—it's my favorite destination when making this recipe.

1 teaspoon harissa paste
a bunch of cilantro, chopped
2 tablespoons olive oil
¼ cup pitted olives, chopped
2 Anaheim red chiles, seeded and chopped
4 slices small Turkish flatbread, pita bread, or
   small flour tortillas, separated into disks

a baking tray
Serves 4

Mix the harissa, cilantro, olive oil, olives, and chiles in a small bowl. Divide the mixture between the pieces of bread, then sandwich the halves back together.

Place on a baking tray and cook in a preheated oven at 325°F for 10 minutes. Remove and serve hot.

top tip: Harissa paste is a fiery blend of chiles and spices available from Middle Eastern markets, gourmet stores, and some supermarkets. It's great to have on hand for firing up all sorts of dishes. Stir it into couscous or mix with yogurt and serve as a dip for crudités.

Bean and mint salad

This is a great summer salad. The mix of beans and fresh mint is very refreshing and clean on the palate.

8 oz. fava beans, shelled and peeled
¾ cup shelled green peas, fresh or frozen
3 oz. dwarf or French beans, trimmed

top tip: Keep a spray bottle full of water near the barbecue. If the lamb's cooking juices drop into the the fire and cause any flare-ups, you can dowse the flames with a burst of spray.

3 oz. runner beans, sliced into 2-inch pieces
8 scallions, trimmed and sliced
a large bunch of mint, coarsely chopped
3 tablespoons olive oil
grated zest and juice of 1 lemon
sea salt and freshly ground black pepper

Serves 4

Bring a large saucepan of water to a boil, add the fava beans, and cook for 4 minutes. Add the peas and other beans and continue cooking for 3 minutes. Drain, cool quickly under cold running water, then drain thoroughly.

Put the scallions and mint in a large bowl. Add the beans, then sprinkle with olive oil, lemon zest and juice, salt, and pepper. Toss well and serve.

top tip: To turn this salad into an entrée, add a little crumbled feta cheese, sliced hard-cooked eggs, or pieces of juicy roasted ham.

Middle Eastern barbecue lamb

Butterflying means cutting the meat away from the bone to give a flatter boneless cut that vaguely resembles a butterfly. Ask your butcher to do it for you—it makes a brilliant dish that is very easy to carve at the table.

2 garlic cloves, crushed and chopped
2 teaspoons ground coriander
2 teaspoons ground cumin
2 teaspoons ground cinnamon
1 teaspoon ground ginger
2 teaspoons paprika
2–2½ lb. leg of lamb, butterflied and trimmed of fat
3 tablespoons olive oil
zest and juice of 1 lemon
sea salt

Serves 4

Put the garlic, coriander, cumin, cinnamon, ginger, paprika, and salt into a large bowl and mix well. Add the lamb and rub the mixture into the meat, making sure every crevice is well coated. Drizzle with the olive oil and lemon zest and juice.

Cover and leave at room temperature for 1 hour or in the fridge overnight. While marinating, turn the lamb over from time to time.

Light the grill and wait until the coals are ash-white, about 40–60 minutes. Brush the ash off the top and put the lamb on the rack.

Cook the lamb for 15–20 minutes on each side for medium rare and 30 minutes each side for well done. The exact time will vary from one grill to another so, if unsure, remove the lamb and carve a piece to see if it is done to your liking.

Alternatively, cook the lamb in a preheated oven at 400°F. For medium-rare meat, cook in a roasting pan for 15–20 minutes, then turn, reduce the heat to 350°F, and cook for a further 10–15 minutes. However, if you prefer the meat to be cooked until well done, add a further 10 minutes to each of these times.

Preserved lemon and tomato pickle

This pickle is great with the grilled lamb, but it also goes well with cold meats such as chicken and pork. You can find Moroccan preserved lemons in Middle Eastern and gourmet stores and some supermarkets.

2 tablespoons olive oil
1 onion, chopped
1 garlic clove, crushed and chopped
2-3 beef tomatoes, peeled, seeded, and chopped
¼ cup sugar
2 teaspoons white vinegar
a pinch of dried chile flakes
a pinch of saffron threads
½ cup olives, pitted
1 preserved lemon, chopped
a bunch of fresh cilantro, chopped
Serves 4

Heat the oil in a skillet, add the onion and garlic, and sauté for 4 minutes.

Add the tomatoes, sugar, vinegar, chile flakes, and saffron. Bring to a boil, reduce the heat and simmer for 10 minutes until the mixture has reduced by almost half.

Add the olives, chopped preserved lemon, and cilantro. Mix well, then remove from the heat and serve hot or cold with the lamb.

top tip: It's easy to make your own preserved lemons. Make sure you use unwaxed lemons and wash them well. Cut 4 lemons in half lengthwise leaving the stalk end intact. Open the lemons up a little and put 1 tablespoon of salt in the middle of each one. Pack them in a sterilized preserving jar, cover with boiling water, seal, label, and leave for 2 weeks in a cool dark place before using as needed.

Crusted golden rice bake

This style of rice is inspired by the method used in Persia—crunchy rice is delicious and makes a sensational change from the white and fluffy rice that we know here. If you want to make this into a meal to eat on its own, add some cooked chunks of chicken to the spiced onion mixture.

1 cup basmati rice
3 tablespoons olive oil
2 onions, diced
2 garlic cloves, crushed and chopped
1 cup ready-to-eat dried apricots, chopped
½ cup toasted slivered almonds
1 teaspoon ground turmeric
1 teaspoon crushed cardamom pods
1 tablespoon garam masala
½ cup (1 stick) butter, cut into small pieces
sea salt and freshly ground black pepper

an ovenproof skillet, buttered
Serves 4

Put the rice in a large bowl, wash it in several changes of cold water, then cover with cold water and let soak for 3 hours.

When ready to cook, bring a large saucepan of water to a boil. Add the rice, stir well, return to a simmer, and cook for 5 minutes.

Drain the rice and fill the pan with cold water to stop it cooking any more. When cold, drain well.

Heat the olive oil in a saucepan, add the onions and garlic, and cook for 5 minutes without letting it brown. Add the apricots, toasted almonds, turmeric, cardamom, garam masala, salt, and pepper and mix well.

Stir the spiced onion into the rice, then transfer it to the prepared skillet and smooth over the top. Dot with butter and cover tightly with foil.

Cook in a preheated oven at 350°F for about 45 minutes, then remove the foil and cook for a further 15 minutes.

Remove from the oven, cover with a large plate, and quickly invert both skillet and plate. Remove the skillet to reveal the rice with its golden crust.

top tip: It is worth having a good ovenproof nonstick skillet. I use one in this recipe and to make tortilla and tarte Tatin. When buying the skillet, remember the handle must be ovenproof too.

Honey and pistachio panna cotta

Here is a very pretty yet simple pudding you can make in advance. If you don't have individual ramekins, use one large mould—an ordinary bowl will do.

1 envelope unflavored gelatin (1 tablespoon)
¾ cup heavy cream
1 cup strained thick yogurt
2 tablespoons sugar
6 tablespoons liquid honey
½ cup ground almonds
1 vanilla bean, halved lengthwise

4 metal or china ramekins, lightly oiled and lined
    with cheesecloth or plastic wrap
Serves 4

Put 3 tablespoons warm water in a bowl, sprinkle the gelatin over the top, and leave until dissolved, about 5 minutes.

Put the cream in a mixing bowl. Add the yogurt, sugar, and honey and stir until smooth. Mix in the ground almonds.

Scrape the vanilla seeds out of the bean, then stir them into the cream mixture. Add the gelatin.

Pour the cream mixture into the prepared ramekins, then chill for 4 hours or until set.

To serve, turn out onto small plates. Serve with the Watermelon and Rosewater Salad.

Watermelon and rosewater salad

Refreshing and easy is the best description for this attractive salad. Watermelons are a special Middle Eastern delicacy, so if you have a specialty store near you, try buying your watermelon there.

1 small watermelon, about 3 lb., chilled
2 tablespoons rosewater

Rose petals
8–12 unsprayed pink rose petals
1 egg white, beaten
1 tablespoon sugar
Serves 4

To prepare the rose petals, dip them in the beaten egg white, then dust lightly with sugar, and set aside to dry for 1 hour.

Top and tail the watermelon, then slice it into thin wedges and pick out the seeds.

Arrange on a large platter, sprinkle with the rosewater, cover, and chill. Serve decorated with the sugar-dusted rose petals.

top tip: When buying a watermelon, choose one that has a tight and unblemished skin. Tap on it with your knuckles—it should make a solid noise, and definitely not sound hollow.

dinner party dream

Is it a birthday, anniversary, or time to celebrate a well-deserved promotion at work? Treat your friends to the best you can offer with this stunning, thoroughly grown-up dinner party. There is no need to feel on a knife edge when preparing special occasion food—these inspirational menus are carefully conceived to create maximum impact with minimum fuss. Pour the champagne and prepare to dazzle...

However relaxed our lives, we all aspire now and then to give a stylish, elegant dinner party with a sensational menu, beautiful matching china and silver, exquisite napkins, swathes of flowers, glowing candles, fine wines, and laughing guests. This is all possible, no matter how busy you may feel. Even simply dressed tables can look absolutely gorgeous and I am sure that the spirit of the occasion helps to bring our kitchen skills alive.

There are a few key tricks you can use to plan easy dinner party menus. Make sure that one course, ideally the appetizer, needs only very simple, brief cooking—a salad or my Gingered Asparagus with Cashews is ideal. Then pick a dessert that can be made well in advance and stored—one that if not cold, only requires a small amount of cooking to finish it off. This frees your mind and time to concentrate on the hot entrée, but even so, choose something simple and stunning that lets you relax and enjoy your own party—an impressive steamed fish with Thai flavors is perfect.

Ginger asparagus with cashews

Fresh asparagus stir-fried with ginger, orange, soy sauce, and cashews, then finished with a drizzle of sesame oil makes a very simple starter to grace the table.

1 tablespoon peanut oil
14 oz. asparagus, about 16, halved lengthwise
½ inch fresh ginger, peeled and cut into fine matchsticks
½ cup pan-toasted cashews, chopped
grated zest of 1 orange
1 tablespoon soy sauce
1 tablespoon sesame oil
Serves 4

Heat the peanut oil in a wok, add the asparagus and ginger, and stir-fry for 4 minutes.

Add the cashews, orange zest, soy sauce, and sesame oil and continue cooking for 1 minute. Transfer to plates and serve immediately.

Spanish roast pepper salad

Mahon is sold in many supermarkets.

8 red bell peppers, halved, cored, and seeded
¼ cup olive oil
4 oz. Mahon cheese or other hard cheese
½ cup pitted black olives
a bunch of flat-leaf parsley, chopped
1 tablespoon white wine vinegar
sea salt and freshly ground black pepper
fresh crusty bread, warmed, to serve

a baking tray, lightly oiled
Serves 4

Put the peppers on the baking tray, drizzle with the olive oil, and roast in a preheated oven at 350°F for 15–20 minutes or until soft.

Slice the cheese as finely as possible (a truffle slicer makes this easy). Put the cheese, peppers, olives, parsley, vinegar, salt, and pepper in a salad bowl. Toss and serve with warm crusty bread.

Steamed sea bass with Thai soup

Sea bass is a beautiful but expensive fish and I admit it's not always available. However, in this recipe you can also use cod fillets, halibut, or tuna steaks, or tiger shrimp. Remember to ask the storekeeper for some bones to make the fish stock.

4 sea bass, 1 lb. each, filleted with bones reserved
1 white onion, sliced
1 stalk lemongrass, chopped
1 inch fresh ginger, sliced
a large bunch of cilantro, leaves chopped and roots or stalks kept separately, plus extra leaves, to serve
2 garlic cloves, sliced
1 fresh red or green chile, chopped
1 kaffir lime leaf or a strip of lime rind
1 tablespoon soy sauce
2 cups mushrooms, sliced
4 scallions, sliced into rounds
leaves from a bunch of basil, torn
14 oz. udon noodles

a 2-tier saucepan, with steamer
Serves 4

Put the fish bones in a medium saucepan. Add 5 cups water, the onion, lemongrass, ginger, cilantro roots or stalks, garlic, chile, lime leaf or rind, and soy sauce. Bring to a boil, reduce the heat, and simmer for 15 minutes, skimming the surface regularly.

When the stock is cooked, strain several times through cheesecloth or a fine strainer.

Put the fish stock in the lower section of the steamer. Fold the fish fillets in half, pinning them with a toothpick if needed, and arrange in the steamer section. Set over a moderately high heat and steam for 4 minutes.

Remove from the heat and lift the steamer section from the top of the pan. Add the mushrooms, scallions, cilantro leaves, basil, and noodles to the fish stock and stir. Reassemble the steamer and continue steaming for 5 minutes more.

Serve the noodle soup in large bowls topped with the steamed sea bass and sprinkled with the extra cilantro leaves.

Chicken with chestnuts and Puy lentils

Puy lentils come from the Velay region of France and have an excellent flavor that works particularly well in this recipe. All the flavors stay in the pan to give a rich dish.

⅓ cup olive oil
4 shallots, diced
2 onions, sliced
2 garlic cloves, crushed and chopped
4 oz. chicken livers, trimmed and chopped
4 oz. peeled chestnuts, chopped
½ cup Puy lentils or other brown lentils, soaked in water for 1 hour
grated zest and juice of 1 lemon
1 bay leaf
a sprig of thyme
4 chicken breasts, on the bone, with skin
1 tablespoon all-purpose flour
1¼ cups chicken stock
½ cup red wine
4 tablespoons butter
1 pear, cored and sliced
sea salt and freshly ground black pepper
a bunch of flat-leaf parsley, chopped

a shallow ovenproof dish or roasting pan
Serves 4

Heat half the olive oil in a saucepan. Add the shallots, onions, and garlic and cook over a low heat for 6 minutes, stirring frequently.

Add the chicken livers and cook for 2 minutes. Then add the chopped chestnuts, lentils, lemon zest and juice, bay leaf, and thyme, mix well, and cook for a further 3 minutes.

Transfer the mixture to a shallow ovenproof dish or roasting pan and set aside.

Heat the remaining olive oil in the saucepan, add the chicken, and sauté gently until golden brown. Place on top of the mixture in the roasting pan.

Add the flour to the saucepan and mix well to form a paste with the pan juices. Slowly add the chicken stock and mix to give a smooth sauce.

Stir in the wine, add salt and pepper to taste, then bring to a boil and cook for 2 minutes.

Pour the sauce into the roasting pan and cover with foil. Cook in a preheated oven at 400°F for 20 minutes. Remove the foil and return to the oven until the chicken is brown (add more stock if needed to moisten the lentils).

Melt the butter in a skillet, add the sliced pear, and fry gently until golden. Add the parsley and spoon the mixture over the chicken and lentils just before serving on a large platter.

menu 1

Ginger asparagus with cashews

Steamed sea bass with Thai soup

Chilled lemon soufflés

Sauvignon Blanc

menu 2

Spanish roast pepper salad

Chicken with chestnuts and Puy lentils

Sautéed vegetables in shallot butter

Plum clafoutis

Sparkling wine

dinner date

Oh, what sweetness a romantic meal can be. Food and love really do go hand in hand.
Everyone can remember a meal enjoyed with their beloved—the place, food, flowers,
wine, music, and words all seem more vivid when your companion is a special someone.
Set the date, treat yourself to a new outfit, and plan an evening to make your love bloom.

Any day can be Valentine's Day when you make the effort to charm your sweetheart. We are all so busy that sometimes the most important person is forgotten, so make time to sit down, eat a meal together, and look dreamily into each other's eyes while you whisper sweet nothings.

Lay the table with romance in mind, using vibrant shades of reds and pinks. Fill the room with fragrant flowers and decadently scatter the floor with petals. Light candles and tea lights, open the wine, and cook the meal. Don't answer the phone or door, just enjoy each other in your cozy nest.

Keep the menu short—this is precisely the evening you don't want to feel as though you have eaten too much—but pay special attention to the presentation. This exotic feast is ideal for your dinner *à deux*: aromatic marinated Chinese duck breasts followed by lightly poached pears cooked with star anise and drizzled with chocolate—very saucy.

Chinese duck breast

Begin marinating the duck breasts the day before your intended liaison. This allows the ingredients to mingle and add their lovely flavors to the meat.

4 duck breasts, skins removed
¼ cup sunflower or peanut oil
3 red bell peppers, sliced into thin strips
1 large onion, sliced
1 chile, cored and chopped
4 oz. cooked rice
2 teaspoons sugar
8 oz. baby spinach, shredded
a bunch of chives, chopped

Lemon-soy marinade
juice of 1 lemon
¼ cup honey
3 tablespoons dark soy sauce
2 tablespoons olive oil
2 garlic cloves, crushed and chopped
freshly ground black pepper
Serves 4

To marinate the duck breasts, put the lemon juice, honey, soy sauce, olive oil, garlic, and black pepper in a large bowl. Add the duck breasts and turn to coat with the marinade.

Cover and chill overnight, turning as often as possible. Remove the duck, shaking off any excess marinade and reserving the remainder.

Heat half the oil in a skillet. Add the duck. Cook over a high heat for 5 minutes on each side, then reduce the heat to low and sauté for a further 5 minutes on each side. Remove from the heat and let rest in the pan to set the juices.

Heat the remaining 2 tablespoons oil in a wok. Add the peppers, onion, and chile and stir-fry for 5 minutes. Add the cooked rice, mix well, and cook for a further 5 minutes.

Sprinkle in the sugar, shredded spinach, and half the chives. Cook for 3 minutes until the spinach has just wilted.

Meanwhile, slice the duck breasts and pour the juices into a small saucepan. Add the reserved marinade and bring to a boil.

Spoon the rice onto warm plates and arrange the duck on top. Spoon over the sauce and sprinkle with the remaining chives.

menu

Chinese duck breast

Pears with star anise and chocolate drizzle

Gewürztraminer

Pears with star anise and chocolate drizzle

Chocolate sauce is so easy to make and complements pears fantastically. This dish looks stunning and can be prepared in advance, then simply assembled when needed—just keep the chocolate sauce warm and leave the pears in the warm wine.

4 ripe pears, peeled
1 cup white wine
4 star anise
¼ c sugar
3 oz. unsweetened bitter chocolate
¼ cup heavy cream
Serves 4

Put the pears in a saucepan, pour over the wine, add the star anise and sugar, and bring to a boil. Reduce the heat, cover, and simmer for 10 minutes. Turn off the heat and let the pears steep in the liquid for 1 hour, still covered.

Fill a small saucepan with water and heat to simmering point. Put the chocolate in a heatproof bowl that fits snugly over the saucepan. Turn the heat down, set the bowl over the water, and leave the chocolate to melt. Add the cream and mix to make a smooth, glossy sauce.

Serve the pears warm or cold, drizzled with the sauce.

Cravings have a tendency to strike late at night, especially after a maybe-too-riotous evening out. On these occasions, warming snacks are the best way to bring satisfaction. Who can resist melted cheese on toast, made with a good strong mature Cheddar and splashed with Worcestershire sauce? Or creamy scrambled eggs with buttery sautéed mushrooms? With these scrumptious recipes you may never phone for take-out again.

Cheese on toast

This is a great snack, especially when served on a big bed of salad including avocado, cucumber, lettuce, tomatoes, sliced red onion, and herbs, all tossed in olive oil, salt, and pepper. I call this a "refrigerator salad" because, however low the supplies of fresh food are in our house, you can usually find most of the these ingredients in the fridge.

4 slices bread
8 oz. mature Cheddar cheese, sliced
Worcestershire sauce, to taste
sea salt and freshly ground black pepper
Serves 4

Toast the bread in a toaster or under the broiler. Arrange the slices of cheese on top of the toast, making sure it hangs slightly over the edges.

Broil for 8–10 minutes, or until the cheese is bubbling and golden. Serve sprinkled with Worcestershire sauce, salt, and pepper.

Farmhouse sauté with bacon and onions

A good high-starch, late-night feast! You could also add some tomatoes cut into generous chunks—don't cook them, just let them cool with the potatoes and serve with a dash of balsamic vinegar. This dish is also fabulous served at a barbecue.

3 tablespoons olive oil
2 lb. cooked potatoes, thickly sliced
2 onions, diced
8 oz. bacon, chopped
3 sprigs of thyme
sea salt and freshly ground black pepper
Serves 4

Heat the olive oil in a large skillet over a medium heat. Add the sliced cooked potatoes and sauté on each side until lightly golden. Remove the potatoes with a slotted spoon and set aside to drain on paper towels.

Add the onion, bacon, and thyme to the skillet and cook over a medium heat, stirring constantly, until the mixture is crisp and golden.

Add the cooked potatoes with salt and pepper to taste. Mix well and serve at once.

late night feast

Mushrooms on toast with scrambled eggs

These days, there are so many different types of mushrooms available. For this dish, try cremini or portobello mushrooms—they make this simple snack look sensational.

½ cup (1 stick) butter, plus extra for spreading
4 large open mushrooms, such as cremini
6 eggs, beaten
4 slices bread
sea salt and freshly ground black pepper

Serves 4

Melt 2 tablespoons of the butter in a large skillet. Add the mushrooms and cook over a medium heat for 5 minutes on each side.

In a separate nonstick skillet, melt 4 tablespoons of the butter until foaming. Pour in the beaten eggs.

Using a wooden spoon, stir the eggs well until the mixture is just starting to set. Remove from the heat immediately and season to taste with salt and pepper.

Cut the remaining butter into small pieces and add it to the eggs, mixing well.

Toast the bread and spread lightly with butter. Cut in half diagonally, top with the scrambled egg and mushrooms, and serve at once.

French toast and fried tomatoes

Children love French toast, which is also sometimes called "eggy bread." Topping it with fried tomatoes makes a juicy, delicious snack. Sautéing tomatoes seems to intensify their flavor and the heat makes them soft and velvety—truly delicious.

4 eggs
¼ cup milk
4 slices bread
4 tablespoons butter
4 ripe or green tomatoes, halved
sea salt and freshly ground black pepper

Serves 4

Put the eggs, milk, salt, and pepper in a large, shallow dish and beat well. Add the bread and let soak for 5 minutes on each side so all the egg mixture is absorbed.

Heat a large, nonstick skillet over a medium heat. Add the soaked bread and cook over a medium-low heat for 3-4 minutes on each side.

In a separate skillet, melt the butter. Add the tomatoes and fry on each side for 2 minutes, then serve on top of the hot French toast.

No matter whether you are curled up with your loved one in front of the television, or working late at home to meet a deadline, a warm and thoughtfully cooked morsel is the most gratifying treat. Keep it simple and savory.

back to basics

Good cooking is easy when you follow a few simple rules. Here are sound kitchen tips you'll want to make second nature, plus advice on shopping and keeping key ingredients, and a few easy things you can do right now to enhance your food.

Let's start simply: every kitchen needs one sharp knife, a chopping board, and a saucepan—then I'm smiling! These are my three basic "must-haves" to cook any meal.

Cheese

Buy cheese from speciality cheese shops, where they are knowledgable and can help you make the correct decision. It is important to know when you will be eating the cheese, so that you can buy a perfectly ripe one for your table.

Meat should look bright and full of moisture. The fat should be evenly marbled throughout but there should not be an excess. Poultry should have a slightly moist skin and a clean smell. Never buy anything that looks dull and dry—it's not good enough for your kitchen.

Buying fish and seafood

Fish and seafood should come from a busy store and have a clean, fresh smell. The fish eyes should be plump and clear, the scales regular and in place, and the flesh should be firm, clean, and bright in color. Shrimp should be firm and evenly colored. Molluscs should be closed or, if open, they should quickly shut when tapped on the kitchen bench. Never accept second best—go to another store or choose another recipe.

Check "use by" dates on pantry food as things do loose their zing, for example spices, herbs, dried and canned pulses, and so on. Use them quickly or discard.

Always buy quality, not quantity
Honestly, you will taste the difference and enjoy the pleasure it brings. When shopping, select the freshest and best looking food available. If what you require for a certain recipe is not good enough, use something else or cook something else. Don't accept poor produce—it will make your cooking poor too, and that style does not exist in my books!

Wherever possible, use fresh **herbs**. Chop them just before use and add in abundance. Flat-leaf parsley should be given a knighthood—I love it. Add it to pasta, fish, beans, casseroles, soups, new potatoes, salads—the list is endless.

Stove-top grill pans
If using a grill pan, always put it over a high heat to let the pan get really hot before adding any food. This will give you the perfect pan-grilled result. Also, don't fiddle with grilled food while it's cooking—leave it to seal on one side and get a good crust, then flip it over and repeat the no-fiddle treatment.

Knives
For perfect chopping and slicing, use a wet stone to sharpen your knives, and use it frequently.

Never serve food (except the obvious ice cream and ice cubes) fridge-cold. You can't taste it. Let it to sit in the kitchen for at least 30 minutes to wake up the flavors.

Be passionate about your kitchen and what goes in it, then your food will improve—honestly.

To avoid a hot, greasy and unmanageable mess, always use chilled butter when making pastry.

The best dressed salad in town

Take a good selection of your favorite leaves, break them up, and put in a large bowl. Add 2 tablespoons of the very best extra virgin olive oil, the juice of a lemon, some sea salt, and freshly ground black pepper, then roll up your sleeves and toss the salad with your hands for 3–4 minutes until every leaf is glistening and thinly coated with the dressing.

Stock is easy to make. The best ones usually contain bones, onion, celery, carrot, leek, garlic, bay leaf, salt, and pepper. Cover with water, bring to a boil and simmer for 20 minutes (fish stock) or 1 hour (meat stock). Strain and let cool. When cold, skim any fat off the top (it will have set on the surface) and freeze the stock until needed. The more jellied your stock, the better the flavor will be. Use it in risotto or soup and it will taste fantastic.

Be sure to wear an apron in the kitchen—good cooks always use their hands.

Steam cuisine

Be kind to your green vegetables and do not overcook them—they will taste much better and look brighter for it. Try steaming vegetables and you will find the difference in taste and texture is wonderful. I am a steamaholic!

Keep a selection of oils in the cabinet

You need a good extra virgin olive oil for salads and drizzling. Sesame, pumpkin, walnut, and infused oils can be used like condiments to add flavor to salads and hot dishes.

For cooking, keep a pure olive oil for Mediterranean-style foods, plus some sunflower or peanut oil for those dishes (such as stir-fries) that should not take on the flavor of the oil.

Buy a good-quality pepper mill and use it regularly. I always use freshly ground black pepper in my cooking—it has the best flavor.

Onions are an important kitchen ingredient, but never frizzle and brown them when mixing them with other foods—it will ruin the texture and give a disappointing flavor.

Ovens and stoves

Gas stove tops are without a doubt my favorite for cooking because the flame can be adjusted instantly. However I prefer to use electric fan-assisted ovens for roasting and baking as I think they cook more evenly than other ovens. If you are shopping for new kitchen gear, my advice is to buy a gas top and a fan-assisted electric oven.

Vanilla sugar gives a lovely flavor to desserts, custards, and cakes. Fill a preserving jar with sugar and chop a couple of vanilla beans into 2-inch lengths. Add them to the sugar, mix through, and let infuse for a week or so before use in your favorite sweet dishes.

To make your own **mint sauce**, chop lots of fresh mint, add a teaspoon of sugar, and cover with white wine vinegar. Let steep for at least 1 hour before serving alongside simply roasted lamb.

Crushing garlic

To crush garlic really well, first smash the whole clove with the flat of a large knife. Hold it flat against the garlic and press down using your weight. Peel and chop the clove, then add ½ teaspoon salt and mash the garlic with the flat part of your knife blade.

index

acknowledgments

The publisher and author would like to thank the following companies and stores who loaned glassware, plates, bowls, flatware, table linen, and accessories that appear in the book:

Bodanova
Unit F4
Kingsway Buisness Park
Oldfield Park
Hampton
TW12 2HD
UK
(44) 20 8979 2929 for stockists

Bridgewater
739 Fulham Road
London
SW6 5UL
UK
(44) 20 7371 5264 for mail order catalog and stores

The Conran Shop
81 Fulham Road
London
SW3 6RD
UK
(44) 20 7589 7401 for stores

David Mellor
4 Sloane Square
London
SW1W 8EE
UK
(44) 20 7730 4259 for mail order catalog and stores

Designers Guild Store
267–271 and 275–277 Kings Road
London
SW3 58N
UK
(44) 20 7243 7300

General Trading Company
144 Sloane Street
London
SW1X 9BL
UK
(44) 20 7730 0411

Habitat UK
196 Tottenham Court
London
W1P 9ID
UK
(44) 845 6010 740 for store details

Haveli Designs Limited
81 Loudoun Road
London
NW8 0DQ
UK
(44) 20 7328 8535 for mail order catalog

Home Place
26–34 Kensington High Street
London
W8 4PF
UK
(44) 20 7937 2626

House
P.O. Box 1748
Salisbury
SP5 5SP
UK
(44) 1725 552549 for mail order catalog and stores

Lakeland Ltd
Alexandra Building
Windermere
Cumbria
LA23 1BQ
UK
(44) 1539 488100 for mail order catalog

Monsoon Home
33C Kings Road
London
SW3 4LX
UK
(44) 20 7313 3000 for stores

Muji
167–169 Great Portland Street
London
W1N 5FD
UK
(44) 20 7323 2287
(44) 20 7323 2208 for store details

Sodahl Design
59 New Concordia Wharf
Mill Street
London
SE1 2BB
UK
(44) 20 7237 6561

Urban Outfitters
36–38 Kensington High Street
London
W8 4PF
UK
(44) 20 7761 1000

Thanks also to OneAldwich, One Aldwich, London, WC2B 4BZ, for supplying the cocktail recipes on pages 137–142 and for allowing us to photograph at the bar. To Ginkco Garden Centre, Ravenscourt Park, London, thanks for donating the plants and flowers that appear in the book. Finally a big thank you to all the staff at Priory Bay Hotel, Priory Drive, Seaview, Isle of Wight, UK [(44)1983 613146] for all their assistance.

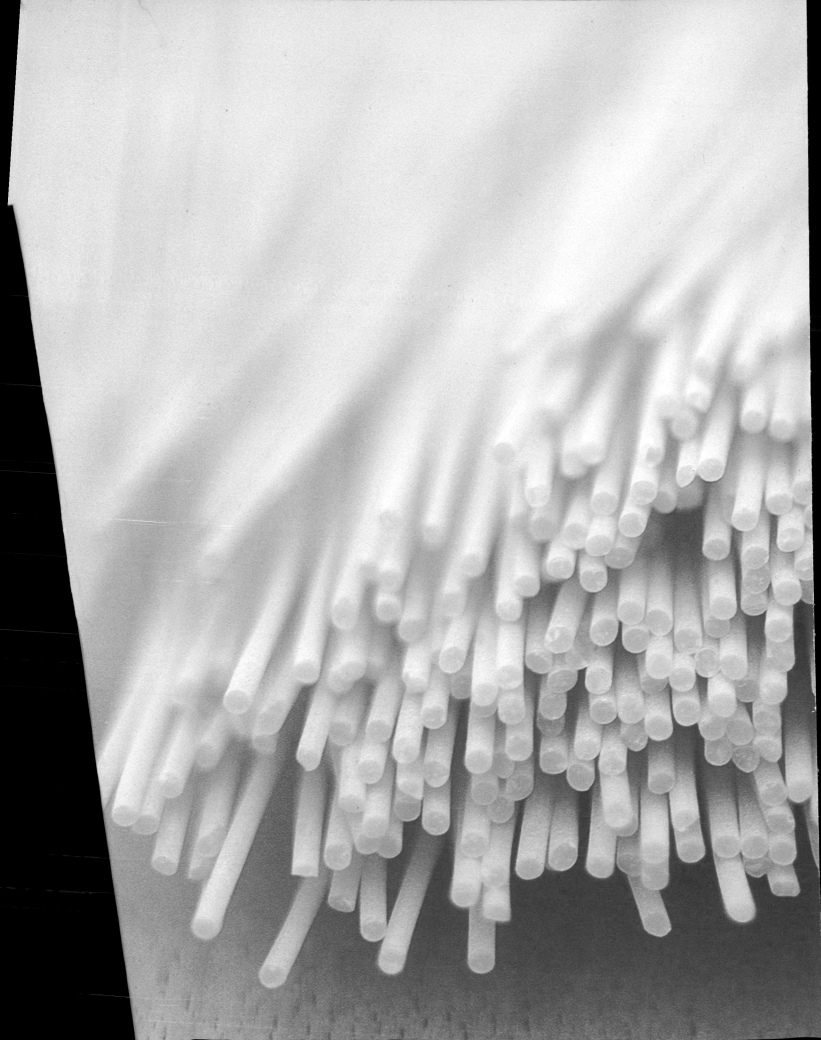